My grandparents, JoAnn and Alfred Wilson, at his sister's farm in Trinity, Texas, in the spring of 1952. JoAnn is quite pregnant with my mother.
(WILSON FAMILY PHOTO)

Advance Praise for *The Living End*

"In a wonderfully engaging heart-of-the-matter voice, Robert Leleux chronicles his chic Texas grandmother's descent into the gloom of Alzheimer's. He is circumspect in recording the many indignities the disease brings and equally faithful to praise the joys of a happy marriage, of good wigs and zinger punch lines. Leleux's writing is as bright and elegant as one of his grandmother's hats, his love of family and faith in their enduring strength a rare and refreshing thing."　—Janis Owens, author of
The Schooling of Claybird Catts

"*The Living End* is as funny as it is heartfelt. Robert Leleux is among the great emerging talents of his generation; I'm bowled over by the beauty of his writing."　—Sarah Bird, author of
The Yokota Officers Club and *The Gap Year*

"*The Living End* is terrific! I could not stop reading this family journey of loss, hope, and redemption. With humor and poignancy, Robert Leleux does a magical job of capturing the beautiful and often complex relationship between grandparent and grandchild."　—Michael Morris, author of *Slow Way Home*

"A fascinating Southern tale of an estranged mother and daughter—and the unlikely fate that brings them together. Affably narrated by Robert Leleux, a man who loved both women, *The Living End* is a touching reminder that, ultimately, we are not defined by our memories. But our commitments to dwelling on the past and resentments can keep us from becoming the person we want to be. Even for those we love the most."
　—Neil White, author of *In the Sanctuary of Outcasts*

"This spare, extraordinary book by turns splits the sides and breaks the heart, but it is the healing vibration of laughter you're left with—what comes when one sees existence whole and luminous, and with it the daunting logic of human love."
　—Honor Moore, author of *The Bishop's Daughter*

The Living End

The Living End

A Family Memoir of
Forgetting and Forgiving

Robert Leleux

ST. MARTIN'S PRESS ❧ NEW YORK

www.stmartins.com

Library of Congress Cataloging-in-Publication Data

Leleux, Robert.
    The living end : a family memoir of forgetting and
forgiving / Robert Leleux. — 1st ed.
      p. cm.
   ISBN 978-0-312-62124-7 (hardcover)
   ISBN 978-1-4299-4293-3 (e-book)
  1. Leleux, Robert. 2. Leleux, Robert—Family.
3. Alzheimer's disease—Patients—United States—Family relationships. 4. Alzheimer's disease—Patients—United States—Biogra-
phy. 5. Mothers and sons—United States. I. Title.
   RC523.2.L45 2012
   818'.603—dc23   2011033803

First Edition: January 2012

10 9 8 7 6 5 4 3 2 1

For JoAnn, Yvella, Mother, and Michael.
And for Sissy Farenthold.

This book is a family story that deals, in part, with my beloved grandmother's journey through Alzheimer's. I cannot claim to offer a comprehensive or representative account of that peculiar disease, and I feign no medical authority. I have nothing but the most profound and humble respect for the millions whose lives have been affected by Alzheimer's and understand that their experiences may differ greatly from my own.

Also, while endeavoring to be as honest as possible while writing this book, I have changed some names and details and, in some instances, altered and compressed time. For whatever errors this book contains, I beg the reader's patience. For whatever offense it may cause, I beg pardon.

xoxo, Robert

Nothing's lost forever. In this world, there is a kind of painful progress. Longing for what we've left behind, and dreaming ahead.

At least I think that's so.

—Tony Kushner, *Angels in America*

I had always meant to write down some of the words, because they were so silly and funny and made me feel so happy; but I never did. And now I couldn't remember them. I could remember the feeling, but I couldn't really remember the words.

Which was not the worst way to begin to forget.

—Nora Ephron, *Heartburn*

Because, after all, nothing is ever really over. Just over there.

—Carrie Fisher, *Surrender the Pink*

The Living End

ONE

The Measure of Her Powers

On the last Tuesday of June 2004—one of those sweltering days of high summer when the Texas air and the Texas people hang thick and limp as wet velvet, and the sting of the heat and the temperature itself both seem as impossible as snow—I hopped the first plane from New York to Houston and beat my grandmother JoAnn to the hospital. I remember that morning plainly because it was the last time I saw JoAnn as I'd always known her. I remember the sleeveless red summer dress that she, always so effortlessly slim, wore when she entered the hospital; and the novel I'd brought but couldn't manage to read; and the battered, caramel leather briefcase my grandfather Alfred carried, stuffed with almost fifty years of his wife's medical history. His executive instincts hadn't relaxed in retirement: He believed in being prepared. Nothing, however, could have prepared us for the following few days.

Once JoAnn had been readied for surgery, Alfred and I sat with her in a stale, curtained-off stall in a wide and feature-less hallway, waiting for the nurses to wheel her away to the operating room. JoAnn's small body, which had looked lissome in her light summer dress, suddenly seemed fragile in her hospital gown, packed away like bone china in tissue paper. Propped up on her mechanical bed, thinly veiled from a row of identical beds by white muslin, she was already floating aloft on a cloud of anesthetic. So much so that by the time I sat beside her, her honey-colored hair falling softly on stiff, crackly pillows, she'd already begun raving about the people on the other side of the curtain.

If the good Lord Jesus had chosen those unlucky folks with an eye toward irritating my grandmother, he could not have done a better job. They were poor; they were loud; they had lamentable facial hair. It was, to JoAnn's way of seeing things, a trifecta of wretchedness that she could not be expected to overlook under the best of circumstances. These were not the best of circumstances.

In some silent, spotlit corner of her heart, I believe that JoAnn had been relishing the thought of this moment, this *Terms of Endearment* moment, the moment just before being wheeled away on her gurney. She had, I imagine, expected this to develop into a fraught, turgid scene, an eleven o'clock number, her own starring turn. From a certain perspective, it was a rare opportunity. After all, in a whole lifetime of Oscar-worthy performances, how many actual gurneys can a lady expect to get?

Another turgid scene, however, competed for our attention. "Robert," JoAnn began, in an artfully wan, parched little voice, "I want you to always remember just how much I love—"

"Aww, now, Mama. You ain't got nothin' to worry about!" A little man, whose wiry, wasted frame I could see through the curtain, began softly screaming to his sobbing bride.

"I'm terribly sorry," I was forced to say to JoAnn, "but would you mind repeating that?"

"Alfred," she started again a few moments later, a bit more powerfully than before. "I don't want you to feel guilty if I d—"

"Do ya hear what I'm telling ya, Mama?" the man, noticeably louder than before, began to howl.

"Forgive me, darlin'," my grandfather said to his wife, "could you run that past me one more time?"

No matter how hard we tried, it was impossible not to be distracted by that wee, shrieking man, JoAnn's new peer and rival, who seemed to be taking such obvious pleasure in his own performance. The situation resembled that of two dueling opera divas, who, finding themselves booked into adjacent rehearsal halls, decide to belt the other out of the audible range. Mere moments before, JoAnn had sounded hoarse and weary. But now, warmed by the spirit of competition, she began shouting like a saloon keeper in a shoot-'em-up Western. "Would you look at *them*!" she hollered, gesturing toward the curtain. "How do *they* always find me? Why is it always *them*? He's as hairless as a Mexican dog, and she's Moby Dick with a beard! No matter where you go, it's the same. He's a Chihuahua and she's the Bearded Lady!"

According to my grandparents, the Texas proletariat was composed almost entirely of whiskerless, whisker-thin men and woolly, well-upholstered women. It was a frequent subject of their conversations. "Look, Sonny," my grandfather had told me when I was a small boy, pointing toward one of these Jack Spratt couples on the street, "the poor man wants heat in the winter and shade in the summertime."

Of course, I was appalled by JoAnn's remarks, but they

seemed to be accepted as a challenge by the man behind the curtain. *"Cain't ya hear me, Mama? Cain't you hear me tawking to you?"* With every repetition, his voice rose in pitch and emphasis, until finally, his falsetto seemed actually to lift him off the floor and JoAnn from her bed.

Waving her arms with a mad flourish—like Tosca, like the Valkyries, like Maria Callas in anything—JoAnn sang out triumphantly, while attempting to rap on the muslin. "CAN SHE HEAR YOU? EVERYBODY HEARS YOU! MAMA HEARS YOU! I HEAR YOU! BUT GUESS WHAT, OLIVE OYL? NOBODY WANTS TO HEAR YOU!"

A low, mortified murmuring began on the other side of the curtain. For a moment, I couldn't tell if JoAnn had vanquished her opposition or if it was merely regrouping. Either way, it was never wise to underestimate little men like the Chihuahua. Some of them possess surprising stamina. I eyed the curtain anxiously. For a moment we sat waiting and listening. And then, through the muslin, there came a low, defeated wheeze, like a punctured balloon.

"Can you believe that things like this can happen in America? And that you and I have to listen to it? A little GRACE AND BEAUTY? YOU KNOW? A LITTLE EFFING GRACE!" JoAnn continued to rant, her strength and volume decreasing, until she finally wound down like an outraged top, collapsing onto her pillow, mumbling all but incoherently, "I can't believe. We actually. Have to listen . . . Just a little effing grace." Then she was off to dreamland.

I was accustomed to being scandalized by my grandmother. JoAnn was a marvelous person. She was not, however, a peppy, "Hi!" person. She didn't care about being nice. "Screw nice!" she often told me. That was the sort of advice my grandmother gave. "Screw nice" and "Get a little meaner every day."

She told me these things because I am (sadly) one of those In-Between People, morally speaking. I'm one of those people who isn't naturally virtuous but who aspires to be—a person who practically never recycles but feels guilty about it; someone who sails right past homeless people on my way to Starbucks but feels guilty about that, too. Hypocrites, I think we're called. I don't volunteer enough. I don't read the newspaper enough. I'm not prone to frequent, spontaneous little combustions of random generosity enough. I'm simply a guilty-feeling person whose guilt does not alter his behavior. Whereas JoAnn was not a hypocrite, and she never felt guilty. For this reason, she was one of my life's most refreshing presences. She lived in a post-guilt world that I loved to visit but couldn't quite manage to live in. "Why are you so mopey?" she'd asked me over the telephone a few months earlier, while I was trying (and failing) to cook chicken and dumplings.

"Mali," I'd feebly answered.

"Who's Molly?" JoAnn asked.

"A country in Africa. I just read a blog about it. The suffering."

"Jesus!" JoAnn answered. "Wait till you get to be my age, with the cold breath of death blowing down your neck. Then let's see how much time you spend thinking about Misty or Maisy or Polly or whatever the hell it is! How many times do I have to tell you, darling, that it's never too late to become a worse person?"

One of the things JoAnn and I did share, however, was a personality that gathered steam in the evening hours. We belong to the variety of person made for dinner parties, a type that reaches its zenith of energy and intellect around the time the second course is served. We almost always telephoned each other after sundown, sometimes talking for hours—she from her chintz-upholstered bedroom at our family farm in Tennessee, and I from my apartment in New York City—relaying news and sharing all our latest jokes and outrages. The previous evening, though, she'd made her nightly phone call with news of an unexpected nature.

"Hello, darling," she'd said. From that first "darling," I knew there was trouble afoot. "I'm afraid I need to talk to you about something serious." She was phoning from a hotel room in Houston, the city we both called home, even though neither of us had lived there for years. And I was attempting to fry chicken in my mattress-sized kitchen. "Not having fun?" I asked, trying to hold on to the receiver through the greasy bread crumbs that coated my fingers. I'd been waiting to hear JoAnn's updates on her annual return to her old stomping grounds. For the past several months, as I'd battered and fried my way through the Paula Deen cookbook, I'd listened as she'd devised rendezvous with all her best girlfriends and epic lunches at all her favorite restaurants. I'd been steadily apprised of my grandmother's military-style checklists of proposed shopping expeditions. I couldn't wait to hear all about her trip, even if I did burn the chicken.

"Well, it's not a day of beauty at Elizabeth Arden, if you know what I mean," JoAnn said, as though she were still exhaling the cigarettes she'd given up years ago.

"No, I don't. . . . Why don't you tell me what's happened."

"It seems I have to have this surgery."

I leaned against the counter, still grasping the Crisco. "What?"

"Now, it's no big deal. The doctor swears up and down I've got nothing to worry about. Only . . . I know I'd feel better about the whole thing if *you* were here. Darling, would you mind terribly flying down? Tomorrow morning? It's an awful lot to ask, but—"

"I'll be there," I interrupted. Because, aside from adoring JoAnn, my relationship with both my grandparents tended, for reasons both sad and happy, to be that of a son's instead of a grandson's. Neither of them had spoken to their only child, my mother, for many years. I was their only grandchild, and loved them dearly. Even if they did *often* make me want to fry myself in a pan of Crisco. "I'm happy to come," I said. "But what's going on? What kind of surgery is this?"

"Yes, well. I'll let Alfred tell you about that."

It was typical of JoAnn to avoid broaching an awful truth. Within the distribution of labor in my grandparents' life-long marriage, bad news resided firmly within Alfred's sphere. Though, in many ways, JoAnn was the most "self-actualized" of women, and my grandparents' marriage was an absolute model of absolute partnership, JoAnn enjoyed indulging in the privileges of her petticoats when it came to letting Alfred play the heavy. In reality, she had all the retiring delicacy of a teamster. But she cherished a filigreed conception of herself as a handkerchief-fluttering belle in need of a gentleman's chivalry. This was a fiction that thrilled my grandfather, as it bolstered his own romantic notion of himself as a sort of Southern Sir Walter Raleigh. While, in principle, I tended to roll my eyes at the whole objectionable setup, as a grandson, I had to admit it was pretty sweet.

JoAnn and Alfred taught me many things about love and fidelity. But one of the most important things was that the story of a marriage—by which I mean the mythology a couple creates about who they are as a couple—eventually becomes, to a degree, the reality of a marriage. We are, largely, whom we pretend to be, at least in love, the part of life most amenable to pleasing self-delusion. JoAnn and Alfred taught me that allowing a spouse to foster romantic notions about themselves ("I was the fastest quarterback in the state"; "I was the most beautiful girl at school") is an important part of a happy marriage. Which is why JoAnn was so ideally suited for matrimony. She possessed a real knack for fostering romantic notions. Nothing was ever quite so good, or quite so bad, as she made it out to be.

So I wasn't exactly shocked when JoAnn said she would pass the phone to Alfred when it came time to talk about her surgery. In hindsight, I also believe she had some sense of foreboding—a passing psychic twinge about this surgery. A feeling of foreboding was characteristic of JoAnn. She was always waiting for the other shoe to drop, mostly because she'd had an epically lousy childhood (even before it was cliché) and was well aware of the perils of high hopes. But I also wonder if, this time, she couldn't help hearing some far-off, existential version of that xylophone they play at the opera to signal that intermission is over.

It's easy to lend false meaning to the past, to assign plot points in memory where they never existed in life. But here's what I can say for certain: JoAnn loved me very much. She often wanted me beside her during doctor appointments. And she seemed particularly eager to have me with her for that operation.

Maybe the only reason I feel this way is because I know how cheap JoAnn was. Yet she didn't bat an eye at my charging the exorbitant cost of my last-minute airfare on her American Express card. In fact, she insisted on it. So considering the price of that ticket, she must have heard for whom the bell tolled.

"Here's your grandfather," JoAnn told me, passing the phone to Alfred while I tried very hard to keep the lard-laden telephone receiver from spurting out of my hand like lathered soap.

"SONNY?" bellowed Alfred, who, in looks and temperament, resembles the top-hatted man on the Monopoly board—bullish, with a white handlebar mustache and a contempt for modernity that began with the invention of the cotton gin and included the push-button phone.

"What's going on down there?" I asked.

"YOUR GRANDMOTHER'S HAVING A BIT OF FEMALE TROUBLE. WE'LL BE NEEDING YOU IN HOUSTON TOMORROW."

"Sure, sure," I answered, noting (not for the first time) that Alfred had a bad habit of phrasing requests like marching orders. "I already told JoAnn I'd be there."

"I'D THINK IT WOULD BE A RELIEF AFTER NEW YORK CITY," he said, pronouncing "New York City" in his usual manner, as though it were raw sewage.

"I'm happy to come," I said.

"BY GOD, I HATE THAT CITY."

"I know," I said.

"I'D RATHER BE HORSEWHIPPED THAN SET FOOT IN THAT CESSPOOL."

"I understand," I said. (Though just for the record, when

my grandparents came to New York, they stayed at the Plaza and dined at Lutèce. Not exactly *Mean Streets,* if you catch my drift.)

"OR SHOT THROUGH THE EYES."

"Yes, but—"

"I'D RATHER BE SHOT WITH A RIFLE RIGHT THROUGH THE EYES."

"But when you say 'female trouble,' what do you—"

"THE SURGICAL HOSPITAL. ELEVEN A.M. TOMORROW," he said. Then he hung up.

Maybe it seems extraordinary that I was willing to hop on a cross-country flight at little more than a moment's notice in order to comfort my grandmother, even if she was paying for it. But I'm Southern, and Southern men are predisposed to mama worship. Also, I'm a writer, and we're predisposed to unemployment; that summer, I was working on my first book and only too pleased to avail myself of any chance to escape blank paper. And, for as long as I could remember, my grandmother's health had reminded me of one of those undetonated bombs under the sidewalks after the London Blitz. Beneath the paces of her life, I feared, the lupus and hepatitis C she'd contracted decades earlier from a contaminated blood transfusion were always lurking.

Part of loving JoAnn meant stepping lightly through the dicey terrain of her illnesses. It meant taking her at her word when she complained of her health, even if she did have a tendency to vamp the scene. Because JoAnn could *Camille* it up with the best of them—posing limply on a recamier with one lily-white hand poised on her brow, just so, like some consumptive out of a nineteenth-century novel. She had a marked

tendency toward hypochondria, and yet I knew she was gen-
uinely ill. I'd accompanied her to scores of doctors. I'd seen
her blood work—her antinuclear antibody tests, and malaise
panels, and recombinant immunoblot assay tests, and other
hideously named methods her doctors had of keeping tabs on
her diseases. I'd picked up her prescriptions from the pharmacy and cared for her during bad spells. So while I might
have smiled to myself once or twice about the pleasure JoAnn
seemed to derive from all the attention her illnesses won her,
I also lived with the very real fear that her health could explode any minute.

After Alfred hung up on me, I spent a fitful, sleepless night
worrying about my precious, impossible grandmother. As a
child, I thought JoAnn carried the sun in a golden cup and the
moon in a silver bag. I continued thinking this as an adult,
despite my firsthand knowledge of her devastating tongue.
Ladling out abuse is one of the privileges typically accorded
Southern ladies of a certain age, but JoAnn took this rather
far. She got away with it because she was funny ("mascara-
streaming-down-your-cheeks funny," in the words of my god-
mother), but also because she never seemed entirely well, and
the constant threat of illness gave her license.

Certainly, JoAnn had never shown much forbearance in
her relationship with my mother. Their chronic conflict had
suspended my relationship with JoAnn, repeatedly, throughout my early childhood. For a couple of years—roughly from
the ages of four until six—they'd agreed to stop fighting for
"the baby's sake." During that enchanted, enchanting time my
grandmother became a regular presence in my life. But then,
inevitably, JoAnn had another idiotic, completely unnecessary

fight with her daughter, and I didn't see her for the next ten years, give or take, until I was sixteen and my father left my mother for a pregnant jockey. (We're from Texas.)

At that point, my mother had what might gracefully be termed a "mental break," and we became nouveau poor. So when I found myself in need of at least one stable adult, I took it upon myself to call JoAnn. "Well, hasn't your life just gone from quail eggs on toast to shit on a shovel?" she surmised correctly, after I'd filled her in on the dissolution of my family life. This dissolution included Mother taking to drink. (We're Irish.) And it also included Mother shaving her head, and then Krazy Gluing plastic hair to her bald scalp. But I digress.

I turned seventeen, and Mother moved to California in order to become a tragic blonde and marry her second Mr. Wonderful. At this point, JoAnn and I picked up where we'd left off when I was six years old. She always seemed a trifle frail and unwell, but we never let that stop us from spending hours chatting on the telephone and tootling about Houston in her butter-yellow Cadillac.

At the time, Alfred was segueing into retirement from the oil business. He'd stopped working full-time and had become a freelance consultant, advising overseas oil-field developments. So for several years, my grandparents moved back and forth between Houston and our family farm outside Nashville, where they eventually settled permanently in the late nineties, once Alfred found even contract employment too tiresome. Then, in the fall of 1999, I moved to New York City to go to college. By the time I did, JoAnn, from her lacquered hair to her Italian pumps, had reclaimed the exalted status she'd held when I was very young. I thought she was the very pink of perfection, all the more precious to me, I suppose, because I was always so keenly aware of the possibility of losing her.

This is all to say that my grandmother's terrible behavior in the hospital, especially given the heavy drugs she'd been administered, wasn't surprising. Alfred, on the other hand, gazed on adoringly at his wife, which wasn't surprising, either. He'd been gazing on adoringly at JoAnn since about 1937, when he first laid eyes on her. He was ten; she was seven. JoAnn Peacock had just moved to Bryan, Texas, and, with her little sister, Peggy, was hanging upside down from the branch of a pecan tree. Alfred saw JoAnn's panties before he saw her face, because upside down her skirts and petticoats hung so low that only the braided ends of her pigtails peeked out from beneath them. It made JoAnn look like a flower being hung to dry.

Like any Southern gentleman, Alfred introduced himself before explaining that he was organizing the New Confederate Army (I know, I know) and asking JoAnn if she wanted to be a private.

"What's a private?" JoAnn asked.

"A kind of soldier."

"And what kind of a soldier are you?" she asked, pulling up her dress in order to square him in the eye.

"I'm a general," he said.

"Good," she replied. "Then I'll be a general, too."

"A girl can't be a general."

"Then who needs your stinking army?" she responded, again dropping the hem of her skirt. Alfred started to walk away. But after walking a few feet, he turned back and, succumbing to her charms for the first of countless times, he yelled into JoAnn's panties, "Fine, then! Be a general!"

"Fine," she answered. "And Peggy can be a private."

Isn't that just the sweetest, most politically disturbing story you've ever heard? Ever since that day under the pecan tree, Alfred had been painting the roses red, which is how I privately referred to his moony, pie-eyed devotion to JoAnn, because the way he adored her always reminded me of the Red Queen's courtiers in *Alice in Wonderland*.

Since 1937, Alfred has adjusted the truth to convenience his beloved wife. When JoAnn lied and said she had a college degree, Alfred said admiringly, "I'm so proud of your grandmother for finishing her college degree." When JoAnn told people who complimented her store-bought jewelry, "These jewels have been in my family for generations," Alfred cooed lovingly, "Didn't JoAnn's family pass down some beautiful jewels?" While nobody could really blame him for going along with these garden-variety fibs told largely for the sake of my grandmother's overweening vanity, Alfred went along with some whoppers, too.

Such as: JoAnn got pregnant with my mother just a couple of months before her little sister, Peggy (retired private of the New Confederate Army), got pregnant with her oldest daughter. Now, my grandmother and her sister had been raised largely by their aunt Kathleen, nicknamed Teen. Peggy adored Aunt Teen, and JoAnn loathed her. Peggy had intended to name her daughter Kathleen, but just to spite her sister, JoAnn snatched the name away from her by giving birth first. My mother always hated the name Kathleen, changed it to Jessica when she was in the eighth grade, and resented terribly the fact that JoAnn had used *her* name as a weapon against her sister.

But, at some point, after my mother changed her name to Jessica, JoAnn started insisting she had *not* named my mother after Aunt Teen. She claimed, moreover, that she hadn't named my mother at all. She began telling everybody that Alfred had named my mother after a character in his favorite poem, which was (are you ready for this?) "The Ballad of Boh da Thone," by Rudyard Kipling.

There are two things about this story that I find incredible. First, that my grandmother must have spent months on her hands and knees, combing through library shelves and card catalogs, trawling through anthologies, searching for some poem, *any poem* with the word "Kathleen" in it, so that she could assign it to her husband as his favorite.

Second, I find it incredible that, like JoAnn's college diploma and family jewels, Alfred whistled right along with "The Ballad of Boh da Thone" in order to make his wife happy. And he was convincing. Poignant, even. "When I suspected we were to have a little girl," Alfred would recite, like a windup toy, "I told JoAnn, 'We must name her after the child in my favorite poem, Rudyard Kipling's immortal "Ballad of Boh da Thone." We must name her Kathleen.' And JoAnn agreed." For years, I bought this performance hook, line, and sinker. I was convinced that my mother had misunderstood the origins of her birth name. Until I found my mother's baby book, buried in a steamer trunk, in which JoAnn had written, "Baby's Name: Kathleen—after my Aunt Kathleen."

So much for the immortal "Boh da Thone."

Alfred loved his wife so much that if reality didn't please her, he'd find something better. It was almost pathological, but it was also endearing, the way this otherwise irascible man was happy to see the world through his wife's eyes, thrilled to consider her every phrase an epigram. JoAnn was often hilarious, but even if she hadn't said anything particularly funny, Alfred remembered that she had.

"Wasn't that hilarious?" he asked me that awful morning at the hospital, positively beaming at his wife, who was positively drooling on her pillow. "Now, I ask you? Isn't your grandmother just the funniest lady? 'Olive Oyl!' Heh, heh, heh. We'll have to remember that one," he said, attempting to rap on the curtain himself now. "Nobody wants to hear from you, Olive Oyl!" he shouted. "Heh, heh, heh."

"Very amusing," I said distractedly, as my worried mind had turned to JoAnn's surgery. It was, as such things go, a minor procedure—to the extent that any procedure performed on a woman of ill health in her mid-seventies can be considered minor. My grandmother had gotten breast implants in the late sixties. At some point the implants had ruptured, and the leaked silicon was thought to be straining her weakened immune system, posing a further threat to her already compromised liver. This was the "female trouble" to which Alfred had furtively referred over the phone. This was the condition my grandmother considered too gruesome to discuss, although Lord only knows why, since I'd known all of this for almost two years. I'd already accompanied her on perhaps half a dozen doctor visits where her ruptured breast implants, and the possibility of having them removed, were discussed. I'd scissored articles on the subject out of newspapers and medical journals, and mailed them to her. But for some reason (and probably just because it made a better story), JoAnn had preferred to couch the news in cloak and dagger, and Alfred had followed suit. It seemed unnecessarily dramatic. But then, everything about that surgery seemed unnecessarily dramatic.

The timing, for instance. I understood the medical reason for having her breast implants removed, but who has a surgery in the middle of a vacation?

No medical necessity seemed to exist requiring the immediate removal of her implants. In fact, there seemed no reason at all not to wait until she returned to Nashville and could consult her regular physicians. Nothing, except the urging of a country club Houston G.P. whose silver hair and silver tongue seemed on loan from daytime television. Apparently, during some recent office visit of which I'd been uninformed, he'd convinced JoAnn of the pressing need to have those implants out. Quite likely he made a dramatic appeal, the drama of which JoAnn appreciated very much. This matinee idol of an M.D. had persuaded JoAnn that though this surgery would be fairly gruesome, and perhaps (at least for a woman of her generation) a tad embarrassing to discuss, it boasted a brisk recovery time. "You'll be yourself again in no time," he'd assured her, with the bright Houston sunshine glinting off his beautiful, blameless hair.

An Unfinished Woman

Who knows what might have been done for JoAnn in those early days after her operation if I'd been more insistent about her condition or had found a more sympathetic ear than that of her posh doctor and his crew of suspiciously attractive nurses (each of whom boasted breasts of a somewhat more than godly perfection)?

When JoAnn regained consciousness, several hours after her surgery, she looked at me with unfocused eyes and asked, in a slurring voice, "Was that a funny joke?"

"You tell me," I said. I stroked her hair from her pale brow.

"I've heard bletter," she said. "I mean . . . bedder. B, b, b, better."

"It's all right," I said. "Go back to sleep."

"She'll perk up in a few hours," said JoAnn's nurse, when I mentioned the difficulty she'd had forming words. "A certain amount of confusion is only to be expected."

But after this "minor" operation, JoAnn was never the same. She seemed dulled and distracted and slightly drunk. It was almost as if she never fully awakened from her anesthesia, which, at least in the first few hours after her surgery, seemed perfectly understandable.

The night of JoAnn's surgery, I stayed at the hospital until they kicked me out, then made it back the next morning before they served her breakfast. Alfred and I were told that, barring the unforeseen, she'd be discharged that morning. It had been our plan to take JoAnn back to the hotel where she and Alfred intended to remain for the next several weeks, until she'd fully recuperated. Just the day before, this had been cause for optimism: *Just one night in the hospital . . . You'll be out in no time.* That morning, however, I already had an inkling that something unforeseen had occurred, that something, in fact, had gone terribly wrong. JoAnn was no less "drowsy" than she'd been the previous evening. When the orderly arrived with her eggs and toast, she even had difficulty holding her fork. I sat in a chair I'd pulled beside her bed, staring at her. Her lovely honey-colored hair was creased and misshapen. Her fair skin looked ashen. Without her fabulous energy and intelligence to illuminate her body, JoAnn looked old to me for the first time. It reminded me of a metaphor I'd heard the great mythologist Joseph Campbell use in a taped lecture. He'd compared human beings to lightbulbs, remarking that the soul was like the filament, and the body the bulb. Sitting there, in my hard, comfortless hospital chair, my grandmother seemed dimmed, her fiery filament close to burning out. I watched her fingers, so fine and lithe, trying to grip a plastic fork and failing. For a moment, I felt almost hypnotized, watching the fluorescent globs of scrambled egg slip from her fork, watching the fork slip from her fingers.

When I was four years old, Hurricane Alicia, the worst

storm of my Gulf Coast childhood, kept my parents and me housebound for a couple of days. I remember the merciless washes of gray rain, the uprooted trees and flooded creek beds. At the time, JoAnn lived in a safe and accessible suburban home, surrounded by grocery stores and hospitals, whereas we lived in the primitive countryside. But in the middle of the storm she left her home, traveling perilous roads to stay with us, all because I was too frightened to sleep. "Let's make a deal," she told me. "How about I stay up all night, in your room, and if anything bad happens, I'll wake you up?"

I remember waking up twice to the screaming wind and the heaving sound of water breaking against the walls of our house. Both times, JoAnn barely glanced up from her magazine. "I'm still awake," she said, in a told-you-so voice. "Why aren't you sleeping?" JoAnn sat up all night in my tiny bed, leaning against the headboard, painting the nails of her long, elegant fingers and reading *Vogue* by candlelight. I slept, all night, curled halfway in her lap.

When I awoke the next morning, the storm had broken and JoAnn was sipping coffee from a teacup beside me. "Well?" she asked.

"Every time I woke up," I told her, "there you were, looking down at me with your sweet little wrinkled face."

The morning after her surgery, after I helped JoAnn eat her eggs, I brushed her hair and helped apply her makeup. "How do I look?" she asked groggily.

"Beautiful as ever," I said.

"My sweet little wrinkled face?" she asked, and barely squeezed my hand. I could see that it hurt to laugh.

Alfred, who had gone to the pharmacy, was back by the time JoAnn's nurse arrived to instruct us in the care she'd require in the coming weeks. I won't put too fine a point on any of this, because some of these instructions were fairly ghoulish, though typical enough. There were drainage tubes involved, and certain procedures for preventing infection, procedures that involved cleaning and bandaging my grandmother's bare chest. Needless to say, I'd never seen my grandmother's chest. We were very close, but we were also pretty Waspy. So, just before the nurse began her demonstration, I started to excuse myself. I stood and turned to leave the room, in order to give my grandparents their privacy. But just as I did, I saw the heels of Alfred's cowboy boots sailing out the door. The silence in the room made the slamming of the door earsplitting.

Without looking up from her paperwork, the nurse arched her brow. "Some men just can't handle it," she said from underneath that brow. "Now, let me show you what you're going to have to do."

It's difficult to put into words what took place between my grandmother and me in that moment. I looked at JoAnn. She stared right back at me. I started to tell the nurse that I couldn't possibly care for my own grandmother in so intimate a manner. I started to say that JoAnn herself would never permit me. And that, besides, there was no way I could remain in Houston for the three weeks (at least) it would take JoAnn to heal. But then, I couldn't find the words. My grandmother displayed no discernable expression. Her gaze was entirely free of pressure or judgment. In fact, she briefly seemed herself, liberated from old age and illness. She wasn't asking me to do anything. She was just telling me, "It's time." As though she were inviting me to cross through a doorway.

Looking back on our life together, this was our finest

moment. We never spoke of it afterward, but when I think over my time with her, it's the moment I always return to, more than the Christmas mornings or the quiet talks. Because, in a sense, it was the moment I was invited to become a man. It was the first time I was asked, by someone who loved me, to do something no one else could do in my place.

"Tell me what I have to do," I told the nurse, who began unbuttoning my grandmother's nightgown.

Later that day, during our drive back to the hotel from the hospital, JoAnn seemed less groggy but extremely absentminded. She twice reached for my name and missed. I'd brought a favorite Louis Armstrong CD with me from New York, to play in case JoAnn got depressed. Like many people, many of my grandmother's happiest moments had been spent in New Orleans, with Louis Armstrong singing in the background. But halfway through "When It's Sleepytime Down South," JoAnn turned to me on the front seat of the rented Oldsmobile. "Who *is* that man singing?" she asked.

"You mean Louis Armstrong?" I said.

"Lou-is Arm-strong," she said, sounding out the words.

Once we'd arrived at the hotel, I helped Alfred escort JoAnn back to their suite, noting, yet again, how he handled her like something too delicate to touch. He trailed behind, barely touching her, as though she were some glorious apparition.

"Can I ask you a question?" JoAnn asked me later, resting on the maroon sofa of their sitting room, the cushions of which were packed so firmly that when you stood up, it looked as though no one had ever sat in them. It was characteristic of that hotel's décor. It was a place intended to look like no place, with rented rooms designed to reflect no particular taste, meant to look like no one had ever slept there before you. In other words, it was dismal.

JoAnn's tone was quiet and confiding, so I braced myself for a "deep, intimate" talk. I wasn't in the mood for a deep, intimate talk. I was scared and tired and careworn, and trying very hard to keep the sunny side up, hoping that it would wear off on my grandparents. So far, it wasn't working.

"Sure," I said. I leaned my head back on one of those firm cushions and rested my eyes.

"Where the hell are we?" she asked.

For a moment, I didn't understand the question. I thought, maybe, she meant it in a philosophical way, like, "Where are we in our relationship?" or "Where are we in our lives?" I sensed we were sailing into dark waters. So I tried to make my answer as vague and honest as her question. "Oh, who the hell knows?" I said lightly.

JoAnn laughed, with a touch of lightheartedness, as though she were trying to play along, but also with a touch of seriousness, as though she were counting on me to be more certain than she was. "No, I mean, where the hell are we? Here. This dump. With the cushions. What the hell are we doing *here*?"

"Oh," I said. I wasn't sure whether to be relieved that her question hadn't been more profound or troubled that she didn't remember where she was. "We're still right here in this ugly hotel room in Houston. Boy, I bet it feels like you've been here more than a couple of weeks, huh? I bet you're getting sick of this vacation. I bet you're starting to look forward to going back home to Tennessee, aren't you?"

"I see, I see," JoAnn said, in a tone of voice that made it clear that she didn't see at all.

From that day on, that's how I talked to JoAnn—in the sort of stagey, stilted language that I'd only previously heard in bad historical dramas in which characters are made to provide the audience with as much information as possible, as casually as possible, as fast as possible, in phony dialogue like "Father, the Nazis are only twenty kilometers outside the city."

Of course, Alfred and I found exchanges like this troubling. But even more troubling was the fact that we couldn't seem to convince anyone that JoAnn's behavior was unusual. *Only to be expected,* her nurses assured us. But they weren't familiar with her diamond-sharp mind.

When I listed examples of JoAnn's new confusion to her useless doctor, he asked straightaway, "How old is she?"

"Seventy-four, but—"

"She's been through a lot for someone her age. Give her time."

"How much time?"

"Hard to tell. But in, say, six months or so, she'll be back to her old self."

"She seems so forgetful."

"Isn't it natural for older people to have difficulty remembering things every now and then?"

The hell of it was that everything this posturing haircut of a man said made perfect sense, as far as it went. Older people *do* recover slowly from physical traumas. Memory loss *is* a natural aspect of the aging process. JoAnn's doctor had logic on his side, while Alfred and I had only our apprehensions. We cared passionately about JoAnn, and somehow, this seemed to emphasize the reasonableness of the doctor's position. He was a professional with no emotional investment in my grandmother's case. He had no difficulty telling us not to worry. After all, she *was* on painkillers. Her health *was* fragile. She suffered from that incurable condition called old age. Given time, JoAnn would pull through. More or less.

For some reason, this explanation seemed less hateful then than it does now; I was, at the time, very young and easily cowed. And it was my first time at the rodeo when it came to dealing with the general disinterest with which older people are faced in times of medical crisis. Since then, I've often witnessed the coldhearted fatalism directed at the elderly. "After all," this kind of callousness implies, "they aren't long for this world anyway." I believe this attitude frequently prevents the elderly from receiving treatment for medical conditions that aren't inevitable consequences of aging.

From the very start, I knew something was terribly wrong with JoAnn, though the only thing that would bear out my position was time. And in a startlingly short time—over the course of a few weeks, really—JoAnn's bright eyes grew milky. Her once confident gait became an awkward, jerky shuffle. She leaned more and more heavily on one-liners and stock phrases that could be used in place of conversation. Like, "You can say that again!" Or "Hell if I know!" Or "No shit, Sherlock!" So that JoAnn soon began to resemble a pull-string doll or a Magic 8 ball, endlessly recycling the same old replies. When questioned directly about, for instance, whether she preferred the tan shoes or the beige, she hedged like a politician running for reelection, offering unsatisfying, unimpeachable non-answers like, "Hmmm. Well, we'll have to really consider that, won't we?"

Like JoAnn, Alfred and I were also confused. Every few days, we took JoAnn back to the doctor; every few days, her doctor informed us she was making a full recovery. Three weeks turned into six, and we spent them in that bland, memory-less Houston hotel room, worrying and trying hard not to worry—until Alfred and I began to suspect that this *was* the process of recovery. Maybe, we came to think, it was like the proverbial watched pot that never boils. Maybe it was like trying to watch your fingernails grow, something that happens with agonizing, invisible slowness until suddenly you find yourself in desperate need of a manicure. That's what we tried to tell ourselves.

I've described JoAnn as seeming drunk, and like many actual drunks, she had moments of such startling clarity and comprehension that Alfred and I often had no choice but to doubt our own perceptions. For instance, down the street from JoAnn and Alfred's hotel, there was the kind of greasy chain restaurant that my grandparents would never have been caught dead in under normal circumstances. One afternoon, however, several weeks after the surgery, we returned from a doctor's appointment famished and sick to death of room service. "Doesn't a hamburger sound like the greatest idea you've ever heard in your life?" JoAnn said.

"The greatest," Alfred seconded.

So I pulled the Oldsmobile into the parking lot of that pokey little place, where we were promptly shown to a booth and began perusing our laminated menus.

Distracted by our hunger, we lapsed into silence. I was trying to determine whether it was wiser to add extra bacon or guacamole to my cheeseburger when JoAnn looked up and, with twinkling eyes, said, "Listen to that lovely music!"

It was a dreary, shadow-streaked mid-afternoon in a road-side lunch spot. I could hear the clatter of pans in the kitchen and the bluster of waiters by the bar's frozen margarita machine. But there was no music playing anywhere.

Alfred and I eyed each other sadly over our plastic menus.

"Hello!" JoAnn said brightly, tapping her painted fingernails on the linoleum-covered table. "I said, 'Listen to that lovely music!'"

"It's very pretty," I said quietly.

"I think it's coming from my menu!" said JoAnn.

"Of course it is, darlin'," said Alfred without looking up.

"I said, I think my menu is playing a song!" said JoAnn. "Don't either of you find that noteworthy?"

"Extremely," I said.

"It's fascinating, honey." Alfred nodded.

"What the hell is the matter with you two?" JoAnn yelled. Then she drew a fast breath. "Oh, my God. You both think I've lost my mind, don't you?"

"Of course not," I said. "Your menu can really carry a tune."

"How could you even ask such a question?" Alfred protested.

Slowly, JoAnn lifted her menu up over the table and rested it in the palms of her outstretched hands. She closed the menu, very deliberately. And then reopened it.

The menu played "Yankee Doodle Dandy."

"You can both go fuck yourselves," said my grandmother. "I have to go to the bathroom."

It was one of those experiences that immediately makes a parable of itself—and as such, it offered two morals. The first: that life is very unlikely. Sometimes, there really are random, patriotic-themed musical devices hidden inside your menu. And the second: that once you've created a "crazy" context for a person, it's very easy to dismiss anything they have to say, even if it happens to be true. Just because someone is crazy or ill doesn't mean they're not keenly aware, sometimes more so than the sane or the well.

For several months, experiences like this provided Alfred and me with little glimpses of hope—tiny, gleaming shards of happy doubt—that made us believe, however briefly, that our suspicions about JoAnn's decline were wrong. Perhaps, these flickering little spells of disbelief would momentarily persuade us, we were surrounded by menus playing "Yankee Doodle" and were just too distracted to notice. Over the next few months, however, it gradually became clear that Alfred and I were not wrong about JoAnn's condition.

When my grandparents were finally able to return to Nashville, we found JoAnn a kind and brilliant neurologist (an Iraqi woman who graduated from Ole Miss!) who began suggesting the possibility that my grandmother had suffered a ministroke during surgery and that this stroke, or even just receiving anesthesia, had perhaps ignited an incipient case of Alzheimer's. By the time these thoughtful theories were formed, they were impossible to test. It was my first taste of something that would soon characterize my experience of JoAnn's new disease—the doctors who treat old-age dementia often seem as confused as their patients. Because, as a disease, Alzheimer's is characterized by uncertainty, beginning with the fact that no one is ever truly diagnosed with it, because there is no definitive test for it. The most you can really say is that someone suffers from "probable Alzheimer's," since Alzheimer's possesses no specific set of symptoms or treatments. Often, folks read over that "probable." Maybe they consider it to be just another example of that "liability lingo" that "technically" alters the "legal truth" of a statement, without altering its facts. Kind of like putting "allegedly" in front of something that everybody knows is true, just so that nobody can sue you for it. I think people often believe that the only difference between a diagnosis of probable Alzheimer's and Alzheimer's is that it's harder for a doctor to get sued for "probably" diagnosing you with anything.

Despite the billions of dollars in research funding the disease has received over the past thirty years—after it mainstreamed in Dear Abby's column and on the TV news—we know remarkably little more about it now than we did then. In the one hundred years since Dr. Alois Alzheimer began researching the subject, no one has precisely stated the difference between what used to be considered senility and what is now called Alzheimer's. At the highest levels of scientific research, folks are still having exactly the same conversation that I had with my grandmother's soap opera–ready doctor. "How much memory loss is normal in older people? And at what point does confusion become pathological?"

As it turns out, no one can say what's going on inside the brain of probable Alzheimer's patients. Over the past thirty years, some consensus has formed around the effect of "plaques" and "tangles" on the brain. David Shenk, author of a beautiful book called *The Forgetting,* describes what could now be called the "traditionalist" view of Alzheimer's neurological progress this way:

> Portions of [the] cerebral cortex . . . becom[e] steadily clouded with two separate forms of cellular debris: clumpy brown spherical plaques floating between the neurons, and long black stringy tangles choking neurons from inside their cell

membranes. As those plaques and tangles spread, some
neurons . . . los[e] the ability to transmit messages to one
another. . . . neurotransmitters, the chemicals that facilitate
messages between the neurons . . . [become] obstructed.
The tangles in some areas of the brain [get] to be so thick
[it's] like trying to kick a soccer ball through a chain-link
fence.

For years, this was the most widely accepted theory of
what Alzheimer's actually does to the brain. But there are now
significant challenges to this narrative because many people
with plaques and tangles galore don't show signs of probable
Alzheimer's, and many people who do show signs of it don't
have abnormal levels of plaques and tangles. As I discovered
in the wake of my grandmother's probable diagnosis, no one
really knows the truth about Alzheimer's.

It goes without saying that the lack of hard science regarding JoAnn's health was extremely frustrating, but on a purely
emotional level, it was also completely irrelevant. Regardless
of the precise nature of the change that had overtaken her,
she seemed to be vanishing before our very eyes. At the time,
I composed a mental list of all the people I knew who could
lose their minds without anybody noticing. It amounted to
scores of bores I'd never heard say one original thing. JoAnn,
on the other hand, had been the genius of the cocktail party,
a brunette version of our fellow Texan Ann Richards, who always seemed poised with some staggering stiletto quip. So
when Alzheimer's gradually became her de facto diagnosis, it
seemed particularly overwhelming and desperately unfair.

Most people would be saddened by the illness of a beloved
grandmother, but I was more than saddened. I was devastated.

I idolized JoAnn.

To me, she was more than a person. She was the embodiment of a sensibility. After all, I grew up in a cow pasture. My father's family, the O'Dooles, had a ranch well outside of Houston, beyond a grubby little town that was hardly more than a funeral parlor and a feed store. Our life centered around horses and cows, and around my father's parents, who were sweet country people. Maybe this all sounds idyllic to you. Pastoral, even. But brother, not to me it doesn't. I hate the country. So might you, if anybody ever woke you up at two in the morning to help perform a C-section on a Hereford having a breech birth in a mud patch. For five hours. In January. It wasn't exactly Marie Antoinette playing milkmaid at the Petit Trianon. It was filthy and it was ugly, and I hated every minute of it. So did my mother, who read French *Vogue* and held Neiman Marcus in the kind of holy reverence Catholics reserve for the Vatican.

My father, on the other hand, was one of the only completely satisfied people I've ever known. As an adult I can appreciate him for the gentle cowboy that he is. But growing up, I resented him horribly because all I wanted to do was move to New York City and live at the Plaza like Eloise. It seemed that nary a day went by without somebody, my father or his father, putting his arm around my shoulder and giving me a big speech like Scarlett O'Hara's father in *Gone With the Wind* about soil—about how precious soil is, and how our blood was in the soil, and that someday all this soil would be my soil. Again, as an adult, I'm grateful for the gesture; it was big and generous and tender. Today I can understand that this promise of valuable land was likely all that these good men had ever hoped to receive from their own fathers. But back then, all I could think was, "Boy, if they think they're saddling me with this hill of dirt, have they got another thing coming."

Enter JoAnn, who was Jackie Kennedy compared to the women in my father's family. She had a graceful form and wore tailored A-line dresses and spicy French perfume. My father's mother, on the other hand—who was, let me stress, a gentle, softhearted lady—spent her days in a duster and a hairnet, watching Dale Evans on the Prayer Network. At JoAnn's house in a stylish Houston suburb, I might have coq au vin for lunch. With my grandmother O'Doole, it was bologna and pimento cheese on a folded slice of Sunshine bread. JoAnn told me to get a little meaner every day, and my grandmother O'Doole told me to take good care of my feet: "You cannot go to Sears and Roebuck and buy a new pair of feet." Even to a five-year-old, the contrast was unmistakable.

JoAnn once told me, "Darling, there are only two kinds of people in the South. Those who use Hellmann's mayonnaise in their chicken salad, and those who use Miracle Whip." It was a terrible thing to say, but like many terrible things, it was also the truth. As was the fact that the O'Dooles were strictly Miracle Whippers, while JoAnn was a Hellmann's kind of lady. And though I saw very little of her throughout my childhood because she and Mother were mostly on non-speakers, the time I did spend with JoAnn gave me hope for a brighter future, and was enough to build a dream on.

During my afternoons at her house, we'd spend hours beside JoAnn's player piano, dancing to zippy twenties songs like "Toot, Toot, Tootsie" and "Nagasaki" and "Don't Bring Lulu." She had a pink telephone that rang "Everything's Coming Up Roses" when anybody called. At restaurants, she'd tip the

band to play "Hello, Dolly!" and then she'd table-hop until
she found a man whose Louis Armstrong impression was wor-
thy of accompanying her. When I was four, she had a red velvet smoking jacket the color of old claret made for me. When
I was five, she gave me a *real* sailboat. Gift-wrapped. Two years
later, she gave me a baby blue Vespa. And because waiting an
entire year for a birthday was beyond my childhood capacity,
she threw me birthday parties all year long. With magicians.
And ponies.

It wouldn't have taken a particularly imaginative child to
envision JoAnn as Auntie Mame, but on this point, my imagination was not required. JoAnn commissioned an artist to
paint herself as Mame and me as Patrick Dennis, with "It's
Today!" and "We Need a Little Christmas Right This Very
Minute" written in swirling script beneath our dancing feet.
As a child, the air was (sometimes literally) thick with con-
fetti and fairy lights the moment JoAnn walked into a room.

So during winter 2005, in those early months of JoAnn's
illness, I felt as though I'd been the victim of a bait and switch,
as though something magical of infinite value had been sto-
len from me and replaced with a sham copy. At that time,
I was probably angrier than I've ever been, and I was also the
most confused. Although I felt I'd lost my grandmother, she
was, on a literal, physical level, right there, present and ac-
counted for. I lacked permission even to mourn her properly. I
didn't have the luxury of retreating to my happy memories
because I had to help care for an unwelcome stranger. I know
it's a cliché, but the one person I most wanted to discuss this
with was JoAnn—who, even if I hadn't desperately wanted to
shelter her from any stress or sadness, couldn't fully understand what I might have to tell her.

To make matters worse, my attempts at writing a novel fell by the wayside, and during those months, I ended up writing the same Sad Sally, saccharine sentence over and over again: "She's here, but she's not there." Precisely the sort of sentimental claptrap of which JoAnn would never have approved and to which she would doubtless have responded with a bemused "Woe is you." But I couldn't help myself. JoAnn's loss seemed tragic, and at the time, I was capable of expressing myself only in the maudlin style of country-western lyrics.

JoAnn had been one of my earliest artistic inspirations. All my fantasies of setting the world on fire, all my daydreams of becoming a Famous Author, involved sharing the stage with my fabulous grandmother. As a young writer in New York City, I'd spent years attending writing workshops, trying to find my voice. When I did, it was my grandmother's. To this day, I've never liked anything I've written that didn't somehow remind me of her. And the fact that my clumsy development, my slow self-discovery, was occurring just as her decline began seemed like a cruel bargain. I was finding my voice just as she was losing hers.

Even though she was in her seventies, JoAnn always seemed like a person with a future. So it was strange and terrible to suddenly think that all she'd ever done was all she'd ever do. (And that, while she was still alive, even her past was disappearing!) But to be honest, it was hard to put into words exactly what she had done. How can you convey the legacy of a person whose accomplishments were achieved in style and not in actions? JoAnn never painted pictures or wrote books, despite having wanted to write very badly. She was, I suppose, what's called a "decorative woman." It's a phrase that's often used to belittle women, but there was nothing small about

JoAnn's power to transcend the drab reality of the everyday, to create special occasions in the face of all of life's blinding boredom. Few people, few artists, can make life resemble flights of imagination. But that's what my grandmother did so naturally. She made things beautiful. She made lovely parties and dinners, gardens and houses and talk. An aura of beauty surrounded her like a cloud of perfume.

But it was also as ephemeral as perfume because JoAnn's real gift was the ability to create atmosphere. That may sound trifling, but it's actually the essential, ineffable gift of a great hostess. The difference between sparkling and flat champagne—the ability to use food and wine and candles and music (unexceptional ingredients all) to create the shimmering, buzzing, whirling mood of a marvelous party: "A trip to the moon on gossamer wings." And because JoAnn carried that gift inside her, because she wore it as lightly as a tulle dress, it came to feel as regular and real as the air we breathed. It wasn't until later, when it seemed that Alzheimer's had already taken everything that was most special about her, that I learned that there's nothing more fleeting than atmosphere. Only you never realize it until it's already gone.

JoAnn Peacock Wilson had been a suburban star in that postwar moment when it was almost glamorous to live in the suburbs. She was that shining lady on the block of whom people said, "JoAnn's house is so beautiful, she could be a decorator!" "JoAnn's dinners are so terrific, she could be a caterer!" "JoAnn is so funny, she could be in the movies!" She had a personality like klieg lights, unsubtle and luminous. More than an actress, she seemed like a character in the movies, and while you were with her, she could make you feel as if you were in the movies, too.

But only when she felt like it. Because when she didn't, she could be impossible. Then, all the fairy dust would settle sadly; all the Christmas lights would be unplugged while she spent weeks in spells of drape-drawn depression, medicated with champagne and Streisand. (She even made depression look glamorous.)

Like so many Southern women of her generation, like so many women of her generation everywhere, JoAnn was a stifled lady. Even though she was surrounded by people who thought she hung the moon (myself included), she seemed chronically dissatisfied with her accomplishments. Because she felt she had to do something, she took up a million things. For a while, she and a girlfriend had an art gallery (JoAnn called it the Drawing Room, which I thought wonderful). She wrote unfinished plays and took poetry classes and redecorated constantly, but nothing about these things seemed enough for her. They gave the impression of being ways of making her feel like she wasn't just a housewife. Or that she was an incidental housewife but that, at any moment, she could burst into glory if she wanted to.

"Sad lives make funny people," JoAnn told me when I was sixteen. At the time, this had sounded like just one more zinger. Eventually, I came to consider it the distillation of her philosophy. Humor was the way she'd coped with every unpleasant thing in her life—she even managed to joke about the onset of a crippling disease. Once, in the early months of her illness, after attempting to tell me the same story three times, she cried uncle, and unfurling her arm like Bette Davis, said, "The wonderful thing about Alzheimer's is you always live in the moment."

This kind of joking kept her disappointments largely hidden from the neighbors, those friendly folks who told her she could have been in pictures, who delivered all the lovely compliments that, judging from the frequency of her depressions, must have doubled as reminders of her unfulfilled potential, so that each compliment became a little jab. You know that empress Elisabeth of Austria? The one who was assassinated while walking down the street, by a man who walked right up to her and silently stabbed her with a tiny knife about the size of a nail file? So tiny that her attendants didn't know she'd been stabbed at all until they got her back to her rooms and undressed her—by which time it was too late, because she'd already bled to death. Her corset was so tight it had held all the spilled blood in. There wasn't even any blood on her clothes, just a little rip in the fabric.

Well, I think that's what it must have been like when somebody said to my grandmother, "You should be on Broadway!" Because let's face it, after a certain age, when somebody says you *should* do something, what they really mean is that you *could have* done something. And there's nothing more poisonous than knowing you haven't fulfilled your potential.

I'm aware that this is a familiar story, that there are many melancholy, desperate housewives, generations of women who could have been contenders. But, until her Alzheimer's, I'd always thought of JoAnn as an evolving, unfinished woman. Even at seventy-four, she seemed endlessly inventive and original. I couldn't wait to see what she might do next, what joke or funny story she might tell. At any moment, she might put together a cabaret act or run for public office or write a breakout book. I always thought she was on the verge of greatness, which may be an insane way for a young man to feel about his grandmother. But this is why I found her diagnosis so devastating. The thought that JoAnn's story was over, that her time was up, that she was being irrevocably drawn into vagueness, was more than I could bear. So much so that there were bleak, private moments when I wished that, if she couldn't really live, she could simply die.

"What am I doing here?" JoAnn asked me one morning as we waited in the lobby of her neurologist's office.

And I had to admit that I didn't have an answer.

THREE

The House of the Spirits

During the early months of 2005, JoAnn's memory began to expand and contract wildly, hurtling her like a shuttle on a loom between the company of my grandfather and me and the company of the spirits. Though I realized that the specters she summoned from her past were merely visual and aural hallucinations, these presences began to take on a reality in all our lives. To a large degree, people and places exist only because we talk about them. But this was true more than usual when JoAnn started talking to her long-dead parents, her aunts and uncles, and Alfred and I followed suit. Not that we actually talked to ghosts hovering in thin air, as JoAnn seemed to do, but we did discuss them, with her and with each other, as though they were living among us. For Alfred, this was a revival. I watched his green eyes twinkle as the forgotten world of his courtship and early marriage came whooshing back to him. For me, it was almost like being invited into my grandparents' youth—into a 1940s world peopled by relatives I would never meet, in which JoAnn and Alfred were as young as I, and their lives lay splendidly before them. It was a surreal foray into family history, a sort of personalized version

of Historic Williamsburg, where costumed tour guides reen-
act the past.

On one hand, it was thrilling, like joining a secret club. But
it was also very sad because for the first time, I felt I knew more
about life than my grandmother did. I knew the future that
was in store for her. A future that was, so strangely, her past.

Alfred and I found ourselves agreeing with JoAnn that "It
is sweet of your Aunt Teen to buy you that lovely dress for
the Cotton Bowl ball." And that "It *would* be much cooler
down at Uncle Hoke's lake house on a sweltering day like today." And that "If Aunt Lela got any fatter, she *would* indeed
shine." We found ourselves talking like this because all of the
Alzheimer's books tell you to "go along" and never attempt
to "force reality" upon a person with dementia. Attempting to
force reality upon people with Alzheimer's was, years ago, an
accepted, albeit cruel, behavioral therapy known as "reality
orientation." Reality orientation did not work. "Going along"
with the evolving reality of a person with Alzheimer's—to the
extent that it doesn't compromise their health or safety—is
now its own form of behavioral therapy, called "habilitation."
This, of course, was a skill that Alfred had honed throughout
his marriage, "habilitation" merely being a scientific term for
painting the roses red.

Aside from being good therapy, habilitation is also good
manners. Because as any Junior Leaguer can tell you, the best
way to communicate with someone who doesn't make sense
is to smile and nod. Ironically, it was JoAnn herself who taught
me most about this. She told me, "People will or will not think
you are a good person based largely upon your ability to smile
and nod." Personally, I can smile and nod with the best of

them. Once, at a dinner party, I was seated next to a woman who thought she was Buster Keaton, and she and I spent a perfectly lovely evening together because rather than telling her "You are not Buster Keaton," I smiled at her, and I nodded. So don't tell me about habilitation.

Another reason Alfred and I signed on so quickly to habilitation therapy was that we already missed JoAnn, and we were relatively certain we'd be missing her even more in the near future. We both found that idea so heartrending that we were willing to do anything to please her. We wanted to accompany JoAnn as far as we could on her journey, to "walk her to the garden gate," as we say back in Texas. If that meant indulging in a certain amount of fantasy and playacting, then that was mighty fine by us. It sometimes felt like talking to a little girl about her imaginary friends. Except the world to which JoAnn had suddenly moved wasn't one she'd created. It was one that had already disappeared.

You couldn't have found a better spot for inhabiting a vanished past than the house to which JoAnn and Alfred moved when he retired. It's a wisteria-covered saltbox perched atop the wooded, rolling Tennessee hills outside Nashville. Built by Alfred's own great-grandfather, a friend and attorney of Andrew Jackson, the house has been in our family ever since. According to my grandfather, Andrew and Rachel Jackson used to stop for tea in our parlor on their way back to their plantation, the Hermitage. Our coffee table is carved from a walnut tree under which Andrew Jackson used to sit with Alfred's great-grandfather and "think great thoughts," as Alfred liked to put it. Which points toward a larger truth: that Southerners tend often to live in a lost past fueled by illusion and genealogical fantasy. It's like one long, slogging Chekhov play down there. In a sense, the first few months of my grandmother's dementia were unusual only because they were so extreme. Instead of leading Daughters of the Confederacy tours of the graves of the "glorious dead," JoAnn sat around talking to them.

A great deal of my grandfather's life, not to mention his inheritance, had been devoted to preserving this past. He was the most family-proud man I've ever known, and in the South, that's saying something. I've said that my grandparents lived in a house owned by my family for generations, and that's true. But though they live in the same house as Alfred's ancestors, the house is located in a completely different place. Longing for the peace and quiet of the countryside, my grandfather had the house meticulously taken apart board by board and, at ludicrous expense, moved twenty miles down the road, where it was put meticulously back together atop a silent hill. The total cost of this was roughly three times the house's market value. But Alfred didn't care about market values. He wished to create a living legacy.

On a material level, at least, he succeeded in fulfilling that wish. The house looks and feels as though it's sat atop that hill forever. It's furnished with the jetsam of generations of Wilsons, rafter-packed with curiosities and antiques ranging from junk-shop tattered to New Orleans fine. Blasé black cattle have to be honked or herded out of the way of automobiles attempting to traverse the long, pebbled drive off the main road, over a narrow bridge that spans the tottering freshwater stream, and gently up the hill to the house. The attics are filled with steamer trunks, and the shelves with forgotten, once-loved books. A couple of Alfred's aunts went mad and died there, adding a frisson of Faulkner to the place.

In general, the house remains untouched by the modern world. It's a place where, whether the phone is push-button or not, the connection is rotary, and those wishing to know the time are forced to count the chimes of the grandfather clock. They're the same chimes that have been ringing in the hours for my family for more than a hundred years—and while listening to those lazy, mellowed tones, or catching your wild, indistinct reflection in my great-grandmother's silver or warped vanity mirror, it's startlingly easy to slip between the past and the present, memory and reality.

Among JoAnn's hallucinations, the most frequent was a beautiful blond child who often appeared to her in the early morning. I thought I was alone in suspecting that this little girl was, in some way, a memory of my mother, but my grandfather must have arrived at the same conclusion, because he began telling me, in early spring 2005, that it was time for my mother to come home. "Sonny," he said. "I think it's time for Jessica to come home again."

If he said this as though he'd long ago banished my mother from the kingdom, it was because, on a practical level, she was every bit as dead to my grandparents as any shrouded ancestor. Not only hadn't Alfred and JoAnn spoken to their daughter in years, Alfred wouldn't even speak of her, at least not to me. A year earlier, he'd even scolded me for mentioning her to my grandmother: "Your grandmother doesn't need to be bothered with all that!" he'd chided me, roughly chomping his cigar.

So it was somewhat more than surprising when he started

saying, awkwardly but repeatedly, during muted television commercials, or over the pages of his newspaper, or just before dropping me off at the airport, "Sonny, your mother should come back. Before JoAnn, you know . . ." he'd begin, and not finish. That's one of the contagious aspects of Alzheimer's. Pretty soon, everyone speaks vaguely about the future because the future is just too painful and uncertain to talk about. I think that's true for two reasons. First, the future starts being measured in real time. According to most books about Alzheimer's, there are, from the middle stages to death, perhaps five years. So, five years of steady decline *is* the future. And second, the future, as we typically relate to it, is a transcendental concept. You know that Dr. Seuss book everybody gives you when you graduate from college, *Oh, the Places You'll Go!* Well, that's the idea of the future I was walking around with before JoAnn became ill: *What will I accomplish? Where will I travel? What will I make of myself?*

But when someone you love is diagnosed with Alzheimer's—or, I suppose, with any fatal disease—the future becomes a ticking clock. Long before my grandmother developed Alzheimer's, she used to rub my head and ask me playfully, "You gonna take care of your old grandmother when she doesn't know which one of the children she is?" But after she was diagnosed, she stopped asking me that. Before, it had been our joke, and now it was our future. And Alfred's future. And even my mother's future, though she didn't know it yet. One of the things JoAnn used to tell me when I expressed surprise at her antics was, "You know why old people are fearless? Because when death's coming to tea in, like, five minutes, you ain't afraid of nothin'." JoAnn constantly demonstrated this kind of fearlessness in the face of loss, and in time, she would also show me the peace that loss can bring, that with tragedy can come understanding and love.

I think that all my grandfather had ever wanted was to be left alone with his wife, but his career in the oil business had forced him to travel tirelessly. He spent, if you tally up the weeks and months he was abroad, what amounted to years in the Middle East. By the time he retired, there were very few oil-rich nations to which he hadn't been dispatched, living out of suitcases and hotels and encampments. It all sounded very romantic to me as a boy, when I was stuck on the farm and desperately wanted to see Paree. And as a grown-up, I have to admit, it still sounds romantic to me, and glamorous, because I've always been that Zelda Fitzgerald type of person who never feels at home in a room without an open suitcase. Alfred, with his cigars and handlebar mustache and old-world manners, seemed like some exotic character out of *Lawrence of Arabia*. But he'd only ever traveled for the sake of his profession, wanderlust being entirely foreign to his character.

Alfred had been raised on his grandmother's cotton plantation in Texas, and his first job, as a teenager, had been as her foreman, joyously working the flat expanses of her copper-colored fields. (Or, as I now realize, joyously instructing black people in working the flat expanses of her copper-colored fields.) "Every Saturday at noon, we'd stop to listen to Bob Wills and the Texas Playboys on the radio," he told me plaintively when I was a child. "You could see a train coming for miles, and then slowly watch it ride away." The longing in his voice was a palpable, throbbing thing during such conversations. "It might have taken half an hour to lose sight of that train, but it felt like forever," he said with a faraway look, as if that train was his whole beautiful past wrapped up in one steam-powered image, and he was still hoping to catch a glimpse of it in the distance. I remember that tone of voice, that look, very clearly, because the obvious pleasure he took in recalling rural stillness was inexplicable to me. It's still in-explicable to me. My grandfather had a lifelong appetite for peace and quiet. That train, that cotton field, felt like freedom to him, just like a fast car on a dark road with the radio blar-ing and the windows down feels like freedom to me. "If I had to do it over," he told me time and again, "I'd stay home and become a land surveyor."

"A land surveyor!" JoAnn (who tended to agree with me about the whole fast car–dark road thing) told me once, in private. "Can you imagine? Do you know what a land surveyor does? They spend the whole day looking through a telescope at something that doesn't even move! They spend the whole day measuring dirt! Dirt! This is a dream job?"

But no matter what Alfred said when he talked about the past, his most fervent wish was that he'd spent more time with JoAnn. This feeling was mutual; the height of their de-sire was to be together. Alone. Meaning, without my mother. My grandparents had always reminded me of those wantonly codependent couples like the Duke and Duchess of Windsor or the Reagans, to use just a couple of overblown comparisons, who're so completely over the moon for each other that it's sweet but also slightly creepy. One of those couples who're so besotted that there's no room for kids, whether or not they choose to have them. Often, they do choose to have them be-cause they love each other too much not to commemorate their love with children. Life is one long honeymoon, but who takes their children on a honeymoon?

It strikes me now that the only downside to JoAnn and Alfred's sixty-odd-year run of marital bliss was that they were so enraptured by each other's company that they inadvertently shut Mother out. It's a peculiar trait of perfect couples that they rarely have happy families. Two's company, and three's a pissed-off kid like Patti Davis, desperate for attention, with a complex about getting shoved outside the Magic Circle.

Of course, my own childhood was not without its ups and downs. My father left my mother and me high and dry broke. She became a drunk and a narcissist with Krazy Glued hair. They were unsettled people groping their way through unsettled lives. But they were also extraordinarily affectionate toward me, even when it was patently clear that they despised each other. The unpleasant circumstances of my early life were mere passing clouds. The ground I stood on, the terrain on which I lived, was their love for me, no matter how pissed off or wounded I may have ever been by their wretched behavior. You know that question hostesses sometimes ask their guests over dinner, "What was the happiest moment of your life?" Well, both of my parents—my untucked, haywire parents, each of them staggering through life with one heel broken—always answered, "When Robert was born."

You can't buy that. You can't quantify that. You can't ever determine the consequences of that kind of love in your life. It lends you a confidence and a certainty that cause you always—regardless of the terrible, self-made messes in which you find yourself—to relate to your *self* like it's a valuable substance.

My mother had none of that. JoAnn happened to be the

kind of hostess who asked her guests about their happiest moments over dinners at which I was sometimes present. Lovely, long evenings spent in my grandparents' swank dining room, in which the air was infused with candlelight and cigar smoke, and the linen gleamed white, and my great-great-grandmother's crystal shone like the eyes of an aging beauty seen, once more, for her great worth. Radiant dinner parties at which my grandmother's fine cooking was the least of the attractions, and during which I never once heard either of my grandparents make mention of my mother, their only child, while relating any of their happy stories. Mother simply did not occupy pride of place in their full and beautiful hearts. Their hearts were, rather, filled with love for each other.

It's always been easy for me to wax philosophical about this, but it wasn't even possible for Mother. The fact that her parents had spent her childhood tripping the light fantastic, without paying her much mind, was not something about which she could be expected to gain distance and perspective. Just as I stood firmly on the ground of my parents' unconditional love and support, she struggled to find her balance on the ground of her parents' indifference.

I'm confident that JoAnn and Alfred did the best with my mother that they knew how, since neither of them had benefited from what you might call model parenting. JoAnn's father was, by all accounts, an extremely likable, fun-loving drunk and professional poker player, and her mother was an oft-married, irrepressible, utterly undomesticated 1920s character. They were both, from what I understand, charming and funny, but neither was fit for, or even particularly interested in, parenthood. At the very first opportunity they deposited their two daughters—my grandmother and her little sister, Peggy—with a woman my grandmother described as a "boring, bourgeois" aunt, the aforementioned Teen.

Alfred's parents, on the other hand, were deaf and mute! I'm told they were kind, admirable people who met and fell in love at a college for the deaf in the early twenties and worked hard throughout their lives to overcome challenging circumstances. But in order for their four children to grow up with a sense of spoken language, they felt forced to ship them off to be raised by a wealthy, imperious Victorian grandmother. How imperious, you might ask? Well, according to Alfred, she entered the kitchen only once a year, in order to stir the plum pudding for Thanksgiving dinner, an act that comprised her annual contribution to the housework. She thought department store browsing beneath her dignity, so she had her maid telephone ahead to any shop she intended to visit, and instruct its clerks to run merchandise out to her chauffered Cadillac. And in the 1920s, she had her postman fired for being a Yankee because she didn't want "the enemy" delivering her mail. That's how imperious she was.

I make this scenic detour into family history only to point out that the biggest thing my grandparents had in common— when they first met as children in Bryan, Texas, and throughout the rest of their lives—is that neither was raised by their parents. Alfred's parents sent him away in order to avoid passing on the disadvantages of their "disability," and JoAnn's parents just couldn't get their charming selves together. They both grew up with a sense of having been radically rejected and without any sense of what parenthood entails. This had various consequences, but paramount among them was that

JoAnn and Alfred were unconditionally, inalterably bonded to each other. Each was the other's port in a storm, the only significant relationship in the other's life. Their devotion, their monogamy, was the closest thing to perfect I've ever witnessed. That's what all their friends said about them: "JoAnn and Alfred are the perfect couple."

I'll go a step further. Alfred and JoAnn were, for me, living proof that it is possible for two people to spend their lives together happily. They were the finest possible fulfillment of the marriage vows. This was true before JoAnn got sick, but it was even truer afterward. As JoAnn's memory faltered and Alfred fought to preserve her comfort and dignity, it became difficult to determine where she ended and he began. My grandfather, a man in his early eighties, taught himself to cook, in order to prepare all her favorite foods, including challenging dishes like eggs Benedict and crème brûlée and rich, heavy bisques. To help his wife dress and groom herself, Alfred learned how to curl JoAnn's hair and apply her blush and lipstick. He took elegant, laborious care of her, and he did it without ever once losing his temper or even seeming to find her endlessly repeated questions annoying. (And let me tell you, no matter how much you love a person with dementia, being asked the same thing fifty times a day can test your patience.) If Alfred ever found JoAnn exasperating, he never let on.

Back in my college writing classes, my teachers used to say that it was "the mark of the amateur" to make sweeping, categorical statements like, "Alfred never felt . . ." or "Alfred always did . . ." because, in reality, people are unknowable and inconsistent, and nobody *always* feels or does anything. But this is the beautiful way that Alfred, and my grandparents' marriage, defied the limits of reality. It's the way that their love amounted to a miracle. Alfred always cherished JoAnn. He always treated her like his treasure. He never tired of her company. And all he ever wanted was to be with her forever.

FOUR

Indomitable Ladies

One is not born a bombshell but becomes one. And before my mother, Jessica Wilson, became a bombshell, she spent her girlhood, in her words, "as a rather lacking Kathleen, just a featureless, fattish, frumpy kid" who, even at eleven, wanted more from life. When she was twelve, JoAnn and Alfred moved to an affluent suburb of Houston where Mother promptly changed her name and set about reinventing herself. It was only the first display of a lifelong talent for reinvention that's proven quite handy whenever she's run afoul of fortune. For instance, when my father left her penniless for another woman, Mother didn't sit around moping; she enlisted the help of a plastic surgeon and started over in California. She's really a Scarlett O'Hara for the silicon age: When push comes to shove, Mother doesn't make dresses out of velvet drapes, she hocks her jewelry for Botox injections, emerging from disaster looking even more relaxed and wrinkle-less than before.

Of course, Mother's love life is often a disaster on a par with the burning of Atlanta, and the latest chapter of her ruinous track record with the opposite sex began on the last Tuesday of the last November of the twentieth century, two days before that millennium's final, thankless Thanksgiving, and six years before my grandmother's final illness. On that fateful day, Mother had, once and for all, managed to yoke and hog-tie her fiancé, and to herd him, roughshod, down the aisle. It had taken her two years to corral and cattle-prod Peter Ickpudth to the altar; it felt like longer, and it had not, to my mind, been worth the effort.

Now, I know what you're thinking.

You're thinking that Peter Ickpudth doesn't sound like a real name, and I'm pleased to tell you that it isn't. And the reason I'm pleased to tell you this is because Peter's real name is actually much worse than Ickpudth. So awful, in fact, that it pains me not to be able to publish it, because Peter's real name sounds appallingly like a stomach convulsion, which is roughly the impression he gives socially, too. To meet the man is to begin gagging and retching. Though, admittedly, it took years for Mother's stomach to turn.

Not mine, however. The very first time I set eyes on Peter Ickpudth, I knew he was bad trouble, and each further meeting only confirmed my first impression. Peter Ickpudth was a cad and a roué and a rake and a lothario, and all the other awful things people say about terrible men in old movies. He looked like the saddest, drunkest possible version of Fess Parker, and he seemed to enjoy baiting and bullying my mother, who, at this time, looked like the saddest, drunkest possible version of Lana Turner.

At her wedding, Mother looked inappropriate but gorgeous. Peter looked as blind drunk as a peach orchard sow. Chad, Peter's wave-chasing, sun-addled son, looked vacant and blank as a plate. And I looked skeptical. Very skeptical. Also, exhausted.

I say that Mother rode herd over Peter down the aisle, but that's figurative, since there was no aisle. There was a harried-looking justice of the peace in the white marble lobby of a California courthouse. There was Mother giddy in a white satin minidress, and, perched high in a curly updo wig ("Look, darling, Grecian!"), a veil that met her hemline. There was punchy Peter in a new, soiled suit recently purchased by Mother at the San Francisco Neiman's. There was an aching pain in my cheek muscles from smiling at disaster. And there was no prenuptial agreement in a community property state—which was, after all, the point.

Or at least I wish money had been the point of it all, because it galls me to believe that Mother was fool enough to fall for Peter. Peter, who was always on the verge of falling over something since he always seemed to be vaguely swaying from hard liquor and hard living and a hard heart. "Well, Mother," I said, "there's your groom. Drunk at his own wedding."

"Don't be ridiculous, darling," Mother said. "Peter's not drunk. Yet. That's just Peter's gait. Peter just has a very . . . nimble gait."

Meaning that Peter wasn't actually drunk at his own wedding, he only looked drunk—drunk being, by this point, his signature look—because by this point Peter had reached that bendy, melty stage of alcoholism where it doesn't matter if you've had the drink or you're about to have the drink, you always look a little slurred and warped, like the film's being played at the wrong speed.

In many ways, that wedding set the tone for Mother and Peter's whole, hot mess of a marriage—drunk, out of control, bizarrely clad, and ultimately abusive. It was one of those lurid middle-aged passages that sometimes occur in people's lives after (to speak in clichés) carefree youth has faded, but before wisdom arrives with age. You know, like when Lana Turner dated Johnny Stompanato, that washed-up old mobster who used to knock her around so much that her daughter, Cheryl Crane, finally had to kill him. Thankfully, I was never called upon to commit a similar homicide, since Mother, in the end, rose to the occasion herself. Not that she actually murdered Peter Ickpudth, but by the time her divorce lawyer was finished with him, I bet he wished she had. What I didn't understand at first was that an element of Mother's attraction to Peter Ickpudth was the baiting and the bullying. Don't get me wrong; Mother's no masochist. She just belongs to that infinitely frustrating subspecies of women known as Indomitable Ladies. It's a type of woman I happen to admire a great deal. But the one really annoying thing about them is that in order to retain their status, they have to keep climbing, like champion boxers, into the ring with men who try to best them. Peter Ickpudth tried to best my mother (even sending her to the emergency room once), but like many men before him, he failed.

Here's the way Mother describes that marriage: "The drinks were very cheap, but the bar stools were very high." I have no idea what that means. But it would seem to speak to the personal costs of that particular variety of dissolute living. For, despite whatever perverse, persevering pleasure Mother might have gotten from this relationship, the marriage took its toll. During the years Mother spent as Mrs. Peter Ickpudth, she was no stranger to a margarita. Not that I blame her. If I were married to Peter Ickpudth, I'd drink, too. But these years were filled with incidents that bordered on the disgraceful. Somebody once said of the singer Marianne Faithfull, regarding her own years spent in the cups, that "though in disgrace, she was always a lady." And that was also true of Mother. I'm afraid that being a lady is much like being a Catholic; having once belonged to either category, one is more or less stuck with it for life. During her travails, Mother might have been arrested and thrown off airplanes. She may have passed out in public restrooms and pissed outdoors. She may have even been compelled, by the state of California, to pick up garbage off the side of the freeway wearing a reflective orange jumpsuit. But she never wore white shoes after Labor Day, and I think that counts for something.

In Mother's defense, San Francisco really is a terrible place for a drunk. It's so hilly. With so many sharp curves. Also, life is not easy for a smart and beautiful woman. (I once said this to a friend of mine who replied, "Compared to what? A dumb, ugly woman?" Which seemed to me to miss the point entirely.)

Who can say how any of us would have turned out if we'd had different parents? Who knows if we are who we are because of, or despite them? It's entirely possible that Mother would still have been one of those women from whom stray men hang like honeysuckle, even if she hadn't model-walked through the world with a chip on her shoulder about having been ignored for the first dozen years of her life. Until, in other words, her chest started to develop. Not that Mother's chest ever stopped developing. Thanks to the miracles of modern science, the lady's been "filling out" since about 1964.

But even though Mother has always enjoyed gentlemen's attention, she's remained largely indifferent to the gentlemen themselves. In fact, she's remained largely indifferent to everybody except me, and that includes both of her ex-husbands and her parents. Mother never joined a bridge club or a sewing circle or a quilting bee. She never dished the dirt with the rest of those dames. She never really even had a friend, except, once again, for me. Except for me, her relationship to the world has always been that of a woman fending for herself.

I've always felt that, in a sense, Mother went in for all her primping to keep the world at arm's length. JoAnn told me that when Mother was a little girl, she dreamed of becoming a secret agent. Apparently, she was the only eight-year-old at Jane Long Elementary School who wore a trench coat to class. So, part of me always wondered if the real function of her wigs and maquillage was disguise. That's the funny thing about makeup, you know: It conceals you even while it's putting you on display.

I suspect the real reason Mother decided to make beauty her vocation was to protect her heart. She's always reminded me of that old joke about Marlene Dietrich. "Come now, Marlene," somebody said. "You're wearing rouge, powder, a wig, false eyelashes, and a girdle." "Yes, darling," Dietrich replied, with a glance down at her famous figure. "But all the rest of it is me."

Mother may have indulged in artifice, from the top of her wig to the heel of her platform shoes. But all the rest of her was real—her humor and devotion, her fierce stubbornness and Texas temper. All of this she'd inherited from JoAnn (with special emphasis on the temper).

In fact, it always pained me that the qualities Mother most obviously inherited from JoAnn were those that most served to keep them apart. Between my mother and grandmother, two genteel Southern ladies, garden-variety squabbles of the type inevitable in even the closest of families became epic battles.

Let me give you an example. When my mother was eighteen, she asked for a wig for Christmas. (It was Texas. It was the sixties.) Among the girls of Mother's circle, the Jody Wig was all the rage, because it was pert and sassy and looked just like Streisand's hair on the cover of *The Second Barbra Streisand Album*. That Jody Wig was the only item on Mother's Christmas list that year. But for some reason (and Mother swears it was just for spite, because JoAnn certainly didn't object to wearing wigs and Jody Wigs weren't pricey), my grandmother refused to buy Mother the wig, and she refused to explain her decision, too.

JoAnn's resolution only stiffened Mother's spine. She said that, without the assurance of a Jody Wig, she'd spend the holiday with friends. JoAnn said, "Fine. Then we won't have Christmas this year." But when, on that benighted December morning, Mother awoke early to slink out of the house, she glimpsed a single present beneath the tree, a Jody Wig, with a note attached reading, in my grandmother's looping script, "Christmas was lost for the want of a Jody Wig."

Thinking about this now, a few things strike me as noteworthy. First, fake hair has played a really pivotal role in my family history. And second, how very strange it is that such an inconsequential, toss-away event could have led to the complete breakdown in communication between my mother and grandmother. As, in fact, it did. After the Jody Wig debacle, Mother essentially left home for thirty years. Lastly, it strikes me how peculiar my grandmother's psychology was. JoAnn could be extravagant in her affections, but she was remarkably withholding when it came to her only child, and in some awful way, I think I eventually benefited from that fact. I think JoAnn gave me any love she had for a child—both because we happened to have a great deal in common, and because I'm a boy and she never felt she had to compete with me. And probably, too, on some level, because she suffered regrets about the way she'd treated her daughter.

This is an adult realization, however. As a child who adored the women in his family, I thought it unfathomable that Mother and JoAnn didn't adore each other. Their story didn't add up. There was no real explanation for a mother and child not talking. I often asked Mother why she didn't speak to her parents, and she'd tell me the Jody Wig story, always ending with "Christmas was lost for the want of a Jody Wig." Or she'd tell me any one of a dozen similar, seemingly trivial stories.

From the start, if Mother fell out of communication with JoAnn, it meant falling out with Alfred, too. "Nobody speaks to my Annie that way" was Alfred's unwavering response to any fight between his wife and daughter. Always failing to consider that Mother was at least as much "his" as my grandmother was, he'd refuse even to speak to Mother until she apologized to JoAnn. Now, I'm convinced that from my grandfather's perspective—that of a man with a fairly Victorian upbringing—his behavior was very gallant and proper, but I feel that it was also terribly misguided. In general, if your spouse and your child are engaged in a chronic, low-grade conflict, I think it's always a mistake to choose between them. In the end, the only thing my grandfather's loyalty to his wife accomplished was the further alienation of their daughter. Anytime Mother and JoAnn had a tiff, Mother was effectively cut off until its cessation. Since the women in my family are impossibly stubborn, our family was suspended for the most trifling and ridiculous of reasons for years at a time. Because of something like a Jody Wig.

Mother, quite rightly, grew to feel as disowned by her parents as they had by their own; my grandparents grew old without the comfort of their families, and I grew up without ever really knowing them, and with a mother who felt fundamentally rejected. I was the most important thing JoAnn and Mother had in common. They were united by their love for me. That's something that made me happy. But that doesn't mean it wasn't also very sad. I was the curtain around which they peered at each other, and it brought me enormous pain that, somehow, they just couldn't manage to see each other.

The winter I was twelve, I resolved to remedy this situation. Mother always grew depressed around the holidays. In the midst of my father's teeming Irish family, it was the time of year when she felt the distance from her own relatives most. That Christmas, my grandmother had sent presents that were marvelous even by her own princely standards. They'd arrived by messenger, which made them seem even more magnificent since, trust me, nothing in Texas arrives by messenger. There was a bicycle built for two and an abstract painting (for a twelve-year-old!) and monogrammed charmeuse pajamas straight out of a Noël Coward play, and a canary yellow armchair, and a regatta jacket (in Houston!), and a huge box filled with beautiful hand-tooled editions of all her favorite books (like Kate Chopin's *The Awakening*) and movies (like *Funny Girl*), and fistfuls of gift certificates to all my favorite shops. JoAnn had obviously spent thousands of dollars and many months preparing her gifts. There was an almost eastern splendor about them. They were like the gifts a traveling pasha might offer a sheltering monarch, which was always the way with her gifts. Together, they made a glistening pile of satin ribbon and silver paper, all wonderfully difficult to open, elaborately packaged, and sparkling like gems. A single gift amounted to two presents: the object itself, and the way it was wrapped.

Twelve was a ghastly age for me. Even by the standard of awkward preteens, I was gawky and flat-footed. So JoAnn's elegant pile of presents—always one of the great pleasures of my childhood—held special significance that year. It amounted to a promise from a faraway star that a different kind of life awaited me—a life in which men lounged about in charmeuse pajamas, perched upon canary yellow armchairs. To my twelve-year-old self, it was the closest possible thing to a physical manifestation of hope.

At this point, I hadn't seen JoAnn in about six years. Nor had I spoken to her, except for the briefest of phone calls to thank her for my Christmas and birthday presents. As much as I wanted to speak to her, those phone calls had always felt rather stilted and agonizing and perfunctory, since with time, we'd lost the ease we'd once had with each other, and Mother, who closely monitored those calls, didn't want us striking up anything that approached a real conversation. "Wrap it up," Mother would mouth, twirling her hands in the air like a morning television producer, if she felt JoAnn and I had lapsed into chitchat. "Wrap it up."

But Mother didn't mind me writing chatty thank-you notes to my grandmother, and strangely, she didn't read them. I suppose this had something to do with how proud she was of my writing. For some reason, long before I'd done anything to merit it, my family began relating to me as "the writer." I have no idea why. But what this translated into on a day-to-day basis was that I had more freedom when writing letters than when talking on the telephone.

So some weeks after Christmas, perhaps in mid-January, I stole several sheets of my mother's powder blue stationery from her desk and, forging her handwriting, wrote JoAnn a three-act play of a letter. I laid it on as thick as Texas toast. As my mother, I begged JoAnn for her forgiveness. I implied that I'd developed new wisdom after having suffered some awful, unnamed tragedy. I claimed to have become a new woman. That afternoon, holed up with my mother's stationery in the guest bathroom, a novelist was born. And then, in a final dramatic flourish that signaled my doom, I asked JoAnn—humbly, but effectively—to call me, so that we could talk out all our troubles.

I don't know what I thought I was doing. I think I must have had the kind of faith in magic that an unconditionally loved child has—that no matter how lousy family relations might become, mothers and children come together in the end. Also, I think *The Parent Trap* had poisoned my mind, as it has the minds of generations of children, by convincing us that by being insufferable, meddlesome, conniving little brats, we can actually bring healing to our families.

Anyway, three days later, all hell broke loose. While I was at school, my grandmother telephoned my mother. (Hadn't it ever occurred to me that adults do the bulk of their telephoning when children are least likely to eavesdrop?) Apparently, the conversation trotted along predictably. JoAnn told Mother, rather tearfully, that she'd received her letter. Mother said, "What letter?"

JoAnn stopped crying and said, "What do you mean, 'what letter'? Your apology."

"My apology to whom?" Mother answered.

"To whom? To me."

"Why would I ever write you an apology?" Mother answered.

"Well, if you didn't, then who did?" JoAnn asked.

When Mother picked me up from school that afternoon, she was trembling with rage.

"Have you just completely lost your mind?" she raved at me from the driver's seat of her white Jaguar. "What kind of little criminal are you? I mean, the theft of my stationery, the forgery. That I don't mind. At least that shows ingenuity. But having me apologize to my mother? Is there water on your brain?"

"I'm sorry," I said. "I was just trying to help."

"Well, here's how you can help. The second we get home, you're going to call your grandmother and explain exactly what you've done."

"You mean, she doesn't know?"

"Oh, she knows. We're not stupid, Robert. But I want her to hear it from the horse's mouth."

As soon as we arrived home, Mother marched me into the kitchen. Sitting beside me on a bar stool, she dialed my grandmother and handed me the phone.

"Hello," said JoAnn. She sounded like she'd been crying.

"Hi," I said. "It's . . . Robert."

"Oh, hello," she said. "Listen, darlin', it's not really what you might call a good time."

"Oh, okay," I said. "It's just. I wanted to apologize for . . . faking that letter. I . . . I was just trying to help."

"Of course," said JoAnn. She struggled to cover the heartache in her voice with a patina of nonchalance, like a woman powdering a shiny nose. "I completely understand. You were just trying to help. But really, sugar, I've got to get off the phone now, all right? I've, um, I've got guests, honey."

"Sure," I said. "I'm sorry."

"Love you, sweetie. We'll talk later. Call me . . . sometime, huh?"

I hung up the telephone, feeling as low as I've ever felt in my life. Mother sat cross-legged beside me and lit up a cigarette. "Jesus, Robert," she said, shaking her head. "You should have worked for Nixon."

Until summer 2005, this aborted connivance had been the closest I'd ever come to reuniting my mother with her parents. And honestly, I didn't expect finer results from the new campaign I began at my grandfather's request. "Piece of cake," I'd told him when, in the spring of that year, he'd first started asking me to bring his daughter home to him. "No problem," I said, quite casually, considering that the nape of my neck was suddenly abristle with cold sweat.

To be honest, I couldn't imagine anything less likely than Mother actually consenting to pay a visit to Tennessee. As I was soon to discover, this suspicion was not unfounded.

"Not a snowball's chance in hell," was, as I recall, Mother's initial reaction when I first started begging her, during long-distance phone calls to California, to join me in a pilgrimage to Tennessee.

Except what she really said was, "Nahat a sanowbawal's chayance in hayall," because since moving to the West Coast, Mother's Southern accent had thickened spectacularly. Like most Texans abroad, it had taken her about twelve seconds to realize the power of being Texan on the public imagination. Texas, particularly if you happen to be a beautiful blonde in a hippie town like San Francisco, can make you a star. In California, Mother's wigs had only gotten bigger and blonder, and she was now unable to cram "hell" into a single syllable.

"You know I love you, baby. You know I worship the ground you walk on. But I'd rather stick needles in my eyes than go see my parents. But hey, darlin', I love the idea of our taking a trip. Where else would you like to go? You name it. I'll buy the tickets."

"Thank you, Mother," I said. "That's very sweet. But the point of going to Tennessee wouldn't be our taking a trip together. The point would be visiting JoAnn. Your mother. Because she's dying. Because this could very well be your last opportunity to reunite with your dying mother in the spirit of grace and reconciliation."

"I hear Oaxaca is lovely this time of year."

"You know, Mother," I said, "when you make remarks like that, other people don't get a chance to glimpse what a tender little heart you have."

"Hmph," Mother said in a tone that implied, with remarkable clarity, that she didn't give a damn what people thought of her tender little heart.

"Let's put a pin in this conversation, shall we?" I offered in my most singsong voice. "Let's discuss this again at a later date."

"Let's," Mother said.

Mother is, as they say, someone you have to love for being so completely herself. And she was both her greatest and least self when discussing her parents.

But during summer 2005, as I dogged her long-distance, Mother unexpectedly started to soften. This was partly because it had finally become clear to her that I was a man on a mission. With JoAnn disappearing a bit more each day, I was aware that my time to effect a reunion was extremely limited. And really, "reunion" is a much too highfalutin' word for what I hoped to accomplish. Of course, I wanted JoAnn's final moments on earth to be happy and fulfilled. I wanted Mother not to go through life with a sense of regret and a lingering sorrow. I wanted Alfred to know that, before the end came, his family was whole and complete. I wanted the same for myself. Much more realistically, I wanted my family to be able to eat dinner together in the same room without stabbing one another with salad forks. To be honest, even that seemed to be aiming a little high, before summer 2005.

One of the qualities I inherited both from Mother and JoAnn, however, is a certain fortitude. I remember winning a prize as a freshman in high school on a report I wrote in defense of Madame Defarge in *A Tale of Two Cities*, who struck me at the time as a much-maligned character, mostly because she reminded me of the dauntless Southern ladies who raised me. I loved Madame Defarge's line "Tell wind and fire where to stop, but don't tell me!" which, frankly, sounded like any Tuesday night with Mother or JoAnn. So one of the reasons Mother caved that summer was because she recognized resolve in action. The other reason is because she was newly sober—freed from her own period of vagueness—and reaching the end of her marriage to Mr. Wonderful. I don't want to make too much of Mother's alcoholism or her sobriety, because there's nothing quite so boring as a young man writing about his mother's drinking problem.

But let me say that only once did Mother ever truly embarrass me while she was drinking—at a lovely party she'd given in my honor, during which her tits fell out of her dress, before she started talking to the wall and passed out in the lap of one of my professors.

Only one really important thing happened at that party, however, and that's that Mother hit rock bottom and, immediately afterward, started A.A. I think she could have put up with any mortifying thing for her own sake or her husband's, but she couldn't bear the thought of really hurting me. That was another notable result of JoAnn and Alfred's marriage. In reaction to her parents, Mother always felt her primary loyalty to be to me, no matter who she happened to be married to.

Mother's newfound sobriety happened to dovetail with the perestroika taking place at my grandparents' house. This amounted to great good fortune on my part, as Mother was suddenly willing to consider any trip that didn't involve Peter Ickpudth. So I was able to take advantage of that sweet, narrow window of A.A. time before making amends becomes a crashing bore. I begged her to visit JoAnn and Alfred for my birthday in September, and finally she caved. "All right," she said. "But damn it, Robert, prepare yourself for disaster! This is going to be just as bad as when you forged that letter when you were twelve years old. Remember, that winter when you were watching *The Parent Trap* all the damn time?"

"This isn't the same thing," I said. "There won't be any disaster."

"Oh, really? Give me one good reason why things'll be different this time."

"Alzheimer's," I answered.

FIVE

The Best Awful There Is

I hope you don't mind my pausing here for a moment in order to tell you another part of this story. Years ago, when I was in college, my refrigerator, laptop, car, and wristwatch all broke in one week—all for completely different and unrelated reasons, and all permanently. When I complained about this to a favorite professor, she shrugged her learned shoulders and said, "Sometimes everything breaks." I offer you that inane little anecdote merely because it's something I had cause to remember during summer 2005, which happened to be another of those times when everything broke, although in ways far more distressing than anything that could be occasioned by a wristwatch.

At the same time that I was observing and helping to alleviate in any meager way I could JoAnn's decline, and Mother was taking her new sobriety very much One Day at a Time, the health of my adored mother-in-law also went, all at once, to hell in a fast car.

I haven't talked about my partner, Michael, yet, but all you really need to know about him is that he's The Perfect Man. He's sweet and affectionate and kind, which, of course, are the most important things, but he also makes a great living, has two dimples and a full head of hair, is a terrific dancer, and always votes the Democratic ticket: How high the moon. As it happens, I've worshipped the ground he walks on ever since I was in high school; and he's made my life far happier than I ever deserved or thought possible. You know the way Ethel Kennedy used to gaze at Bobby, like he was Christ with a cute haircut? Well, that's exactly the way I find myself looking at Michael: I have to pinch myself to know he's for real. He also happens to have a wonderful mother, Yvella "Call Me Mom" Leleux, who made a point of loving me the moment Michael told her he did, and has treated me, since I was seventeen years old, with as much warmth and kindness as if she'd given birth to me. It is what's called a blessing.

The first time I ever saw Yvella Leleux I was seventeen years old. I was standing in the entry of her house—a broad, rambling residence as English Tudor as anyplace in Houston, Texas—and she was standing at the head of her staircase, carrying a basket of mending. Because I'd just read *Howards End,* she reminded me of Mrs. Wilcox, the graceful, long-skirted lady who embodies the spirit of home so central to that book. I'd been bashful about meeting Michael's mother. From his description of her, the one thing I knew for certain about Yvella Leleux was that she was devout, and the one thing I was certain Yvella would know immediately about me was that I was crazy in love with her son and I wasn't at all certain how compatible these two bits of information would prove to be. At that age, I was often able, when in the company of strangers, only to shift between two excruciating gears in my personality: I was either unbearably sheepish, to the point of finding direct eye contact agonizing, or I was almost superhumanly brassy, like some thirties spit-curled chorine. With Michael's mother, on that day of our first meeting, I was both. To her great and lasting credit, she paid attention to neither.

When Mom reached the bottom of the stairs—its banister wobbly and carpet spotted from two generations of children—she handed her basket off to Michael and, forcing me to meet her eye, said, "Now, you must be Robert. Michael's told me so many wonderful things about you."

I could barely stammer out a polite response. "Oh, thanks," I said. "Likewise."

Mom's smile moved from me to Michael. She tucked a heavy lock of her dark hair behind a shapely ear. "I know the family is dying to meet you. Everyone should be in the family room. Do you two have a minute?" she asked in a coaxing tone that one might use with a saddle-shy horse or skittish child.

"Sure," said Michael. "If Robert . . ."

"Well . . ." I said.

"Terrific," said Mom. Linking her arm with mine, she marshaled me into the family room. It was a room in which everyone was not, of course, dying to meet me. But it was also a room in which everyone—for the moment, anyway—pretended they were, because I was flying under the wing of Mom's maternal authority. "Everybody," Mom said, "this is Michael's new . . . friend, Robert." She eyed the room steadily, like an Old West sheriff staring down a bandit-crammed corral. "Who's staying for supper?"

At the end of that supper—a meal that was, by turns, like so many significant beginnings, painfully awkward, yet strangely familiar—Mom walked us through the inky blue Houston evening toward Michael's jalopy. I piled the cellophaned plates of leftovers she'd foisted upon us onto the car's shabby, collapsing upholstery, then turned to shake her hand. But she pushed aside my outstretched arm and hugged me. "I'm so happy you came here tonight," she said softly. "And I'm so happy you decided to stay for supper." I was embarrassed by the openness of her affection, but also deeply touched. And so, dashing from excruciating shyness to crazed overconfidence, I seized her by the shoulders and said, "When you get very old, I promise to take care of you. And when you go blind and senile, I promise not to dye your hair any humiliating color just so strangers can make fun of you." At the time, I think I thought this was the kind of "unconventional" dialogue my character would say to Yvella's character in the movie version of our lives.

Mom stepped back slightly and raised her hand to conceal a rather bemused grin. "Well, I'm sure I'll really appreciate that," she said. "When the time comes. In fact, I'll hold you to it." Then, turning to Michael, she said, "Get him home safe, honey, okay? This one's a keeper."

I'm not sure what I'd done to earn "keeper" status, but that warm winter evening was the start of a beautiful friendship between Yvella and me. From the very beginning, no matter how wrong I was, I could do no wrong with her.

In summer 2005, Michael—who'd been incredibly patient about my flying back and forth to Nashville whenever JoAnn had an important doctor's appointment or Alfred needed reinforcements—expressed the very reasonable desire of spending his vacation with his own family in Houston. I happily agreed. Not only had Michael endured an unearthly number of holidays with my grandparents (who adored him, by the way), but the idea of a little rest and relaxation in the Texas sun-shine sounded mighty fine to me, too. The thought of Yvella's (now my mother-in-law's) cooking didn't sound bad, either, as it tended wonderfully toward starches and fried goods and was, consequently, delicious.

But on our very first day back in Houston—after a morn-ing spent cruising the supermarket aisles for Crisco and Con-federate sugar—we returned to the Leleuxs' sprawling suburban house to find Yvella collapsed on the floor of her bedroom, having suffered a major stroke. Perhaps five minutes earlier, Michael and I'd been loading the trunk of Mom's mammoth Lincoln with brown paper bags brimming with carbohydrates when she'd phoned Michael to say, in a halting, stammering voice, "Would you mind heading back to the house now? I'm suddenly not feeling too well." Michael sped the Lincoln back to the house, but by the time we arrived, she'd already stopped breathing. I called 911. A team of paramedics seemed to materialize out of thin air. They proceeded to jolt Mom— the tenderest person I've ever known—horribly back to life. I forced myself to look away, and when I did, I noticed that two of our nieces, neither more than six, had crept silently into the room. They stood stock-still, staring at the awful, weighty, flour-sack quality Mom's body had suddenly devel-oped, and at her ancient, love-worn velvet dressing gown be-ing torn from her chest to clear the way for the brutal workings of the paramedics. The little girls looked too stricken to cry. It was somehow so primally terrifying to see this gen-tle woman, who'd given life to us all in one way or another, reduced to this misfiring body, trembling and jerking and unresponsive.

Without thinking, I scooped up the nieces, deposited them

in front of a television upstairs, and proceeded to lie my head off in a manner I found objectionable even at the time— assuring the girls that everything was going to be just fine; that Grandma was going to be just fine; that they shouldn't worry about a thing, and should, instead, watch cartoons and avoid, under any circumstances, coming downstairs until someone fetched them. And then I left them in front of that TV set, its sounds and colors ringing violently off the walls.

Some fifteen minutes later, Mom was taken in an ambulance to a suburban "satellite" hospital, where the staff quickly declared themselves incapable of coping with her condition. She was life-flighted to the Methodist Hospital downtown, where she remained for the next four days, alive but unconscious. During that time, Michael never left his mother's side. He slept in a chair beside her bed. He talked to her, read to her, told her jokes and stories. He sang her all the lullabies she'd once sung to him. The nurses—lovely people all, including one remarkable Indian woman who insisted upon demonstrating her yoga positions, then invited us to attend her megachurch—were kind but pragmatic, and cautioned us that, due to loss of oxygen to the brain immediately following her stroke, Mom would almost certainly suffer some degree of brain damage, if she regained consciousness at all. Of course, it's the job of health professionals, like theatrical agents and stockbrokers, to "manage expectations," but sharing this grim warning only served to quell any glimmer of hope we might have had about Mom's recovery and only added suspense and anxiety to those endless, molasses-paced days, so that we came to feel that what we were waiting for might turn out to be even worse than what we were already experiencing.

Throughout this whole hideous time, I tried to make myself as useful as possible in the way I know best: shopping. I made Starbucks and fast-food runs. I brought the family fresh shirts and doughnuts. I bought so many brainless gossip rags that I now firmly believe that I personally forestalled the collapse of print media by at least several months. I also tried (a great trial for me) to be quiet and offer my opinion as rarely as possible, in order to respect the fact that, though I was heartbroken about Mom, this was the particular tragedy of Michael and his sisters. If I may offer a word of advice to any in-law, man or woman, who wishes to be supportive during a time of crisis, it's this: Shut up. Shut up, and fetch as many cups of coffee and copies of the *National Enquirer* as may be desired by your spouse's family.

On the fifth day, Mom mercifully awoke, just as Michael was reeling off the astounding history of her blood pressure medication (think Gibbon's *Decline and Fall*) to her doctor. "Diprovan," Michael said, wrongly as it turns out. At which point, Mom, whom everyone still believed to be comatose, slowly lifted her right hand, and amidst her children's cries of joy and relief, shakily spelled the correct name of her medication in the air with her index finger: "D-I-O-V-A-N." "Diovan!" Michael shouted to his sisters. "Mom wrote Diovan! She heard me say Diprovan, but it isn't Diprovan! It was never Diprovan! It was Diovan all along, and she knew it, and so she wrote it in the air with her finger!" "Hooray!" we all shouted. "Hooray for Mom! Hooray for Diovan!" (Which really just goes to show how relative happiness can be.) Mom managed to flash a weak, fleeting grin of satisfaction. "I think she's going to make a full recovery," the doctor deadpanned.

Mom *was* going to make a full recovery, give or take. Miraculously, she'd suffered no brain damage or paralysis—though she had permanently lost broad swaths of her peripheral vision. At first, it was difficult for her even to turn her head. She couldn't feed herself or speak. Standing and walking were utterly beyond her. Over the next several months, she slowly regained her strength, but during much of those months, she was weak as a kitten and in obvious physical pain.

Though the hospital staff was heroic, they couldn't be expected to provide the sort of personal attention that Mom (a woman who, even when in finest fettle, insists upon a standard of comfort straight out of "The Princess and the Pea") requires. It was clear that somebody in our big Catholic family would need to stay to watch over her. But after a couple of weeks, Michael had to head back to his New York power job, and my sisters-in-law to their young children. I, however, was footloose that summer. Aside from my faint, frustrated dreams of being a writer, the only pressing business I had was JoAnn's declining health. Out of Michael's entire family, I was the only grown-up with time on his hands.

So for the next month, I lived in a beige vinyl recliner in Mom's hospital room, doing whatever paltry thing I could to make her more comfortable. You know that great Robert Hayden poem that ends with the line "What did I know, what did I know of love's austere and lonely offices?" Well, as it turns out, I knew bubkes (as we say in East Texas). But in my totally inadequate fashion, I tried to offer Mom an infinitesimal return on the expert care she'd given me so freely over the years. Mostly, it was just fetching ice shavings and pillow plumping and brushing her beautiful dark hair—anything to lessen the pain that was so terrible to witness. Though not so terrible as watching her question the imperative of her recovery. She seemed ensnared in her body, but more than that, she seemed stranded in her life.

Yvella Cormier dropped out of the eighth grade when she was fourteen years old *(fourteen!)* to marry Michael's father, Chester Leleux. At nineteen, she had her first baby, and over the next twenty-one years, she had three more, plus two miscarriages.

Shortly after her last child began elementary school, her husband had his second heart attack and was forced to retire early from a commendable career in the oil business. Dad was more or less housebound for the rest of his life, suffering from heart trouble and a debilitating depression, and requiring constant care—so that the retirement that was forced upon Chester denied Yvella her own. Then, of course, the oldest children started having children. Mom was one of those venerable Catholic ladies whose whole adult lives are spent in service to their families, handed over to them completely. Women who're overwhelmed by their own sense of duty and generosity—by measles and dance recitals and Halloween costumes and male ego stroking.

Mom never joined a ladies auxiliary. She never learned how to fox-trot or the Italian word for window. She never even read the Book of the Month. She is, quite simply, the most selfless, exhausted person I've ever known. She didn't complain about it, but that's not to say she didn't acknowledge it. "I sacrificed my whole life for my family," she often said, without bitterness, really, but with a sort of awe at the completeness of the statement. That's also not to say that she hadn't wanted more, that she hadn't looked forward to a retirement that never came, one filled with unfulfilled fantasies of cruise ships and ballroom dancing and time to draw! To paint! The closets of her house were filled with sketchbooks—with her pleasant, pleasing drawings of children and flowers. For years, she'd illustrated the programs of her children's dance recitals, all their school projects. "Nobody's going to recognize me," she'd assured Michael and me, when we begged her to visit us in New York, or at least her sisters back in Louisiana. "As soon as Dad gets better . . ." or "As soon as the kids get a little older . . ." she'd tell us, "I'll do all those things. I tell you, nobody's going to even recognize my life."

But then, during an unbelievable spell of bad luck, Mom—who'd run her health down terribly in the final years of Chester's illness, rarely leaving his sickroom even to go to the supermarket or pharmacy—had her first stroke and then a triple bypass in summer 2002, just three days before her husband died. She spent the day of his funeral in the same hospital where he'd so often received treatment, being tended to by the same doctors who'd cared for him. By the time Mom was allowed to return home, Dad was gone forever.

Upon his death, the annuity that comprised the lion's share of her income was halved, leaving her with what's often so charmingly referred to as "a widow's pension." She couldn't afford to keep the home where she'd raised her family and, worse still, her children weren't around to justify its expense. With Michael and his sisters scattered across the country, Mom seemed to have been defeated by her own success—she'd devoted her life to her family, supported them without reservation, helped to establish them in the world, and now what? In the third act of a selfless life, she was left alone with a sense of despair and loss, and with the daunting prospect of an uphill recovery.

During the three years following Dad's death, Michael and

I worked very hard to rouse Mom out of the doldrums—dragging her to New York, where in one wonderful week, we painted the town. We saw Bobby Short at the Café Carlyle, dined at the Plaza, attended one Broadway play after the next. We begged her to live with us. But Mom never felt quite well. She was haunted by money worries, and what's more, she'd never developed the habit of independence. Left to her own devices, it turned out she didn't have any. Yvella was, in a sense, still a fourteen-year-old girl who'd never been brought out or developed. Chester Leleux had been an affectionate, loving husband who'd taken such exquisite care of his wife that he'd inadvertently infantilized her. Michael tells a story about crossing the street with Mom one day, and when the sign started flashing DON'T WALK, she stopped walking right in the middle of the street. Mom didn't know how to pay the electric bill or balance her checkbook or pump gas. She was completely unprepared to live alone, and in many ways, it was too late for her to learn. Her situation reminded me, sadly, of that famous speech by Elizabeth Cady Stanton, "The Solitude of Self," in which she warns, "No matter how much women prefer to lean, to be protected and supported, nor how much men desire to have them do so, they must make the voyage of life alone." It was now time for Mom to captain her own ship, to chart her course, to, as Stanton says, "match the wind and waves and . . . read the signs in the firmament over all." As hard as she could, Mom was trying to steer her little boat through the hour of danger, only nobody had ever taught her how to handle the oars.

During the time I spent with Yvella in summer 2005, she seemed so frightened about the future, uncertain as to how to proceed in her life, and saddled with pain and unpaid bills. "I'm trying to figure out just what I should do now," she kept saying, tearfully. "There has to be a way I can figure all this out." Of course, part of this sadness was the situational depression that often accompanies recovery from a major illness. But another part was just sound good sense. Yvella didn't want to move in with her children or into a retirement home, but she couldn't afford to live alone, nor was she physically capable of caring for herself. And neither I nor Michael and his sisters had any idea how to advise her.

It seemed incredible to me how few options she had. Or any older person, for that matter—scarcely more than had been available fifty or a hundred years ago. It sometimes seems that modern science and the democratizing reforms in government have utterly transformed every part of life in the past century— from conception through childhood, adolescence through adulthood—except old age! Think of artificial insemination, the birth control pill, early childhood education, the polio vaccine, penicillin, universal suffrage, reproductive choice, the forty-hour workweek, mammograms, Viagra, pacemakers! The first sixty-odd years of life little resemble the stark realities of the nineteenth century, but after that, human progress seems to peter out. Sure, there's Medicare and Social Security, both marvelous things. But as far as the way life is lived by the elderly, the choices faced by the old and infirm, like whether to move in with your children or take your chances with a public home, the options are slim pickins indeed.

Pondering Yvella's dilemma gave me new perspective on JoAnn. For the first time, I realized how much I'd allowed my own grief and fear to color the way I considered her

Alzheimer's. For my grandfather and me, having to witness
JoAnn's decline was agonizing—like watching *The Miracle
Worker* backward, every day accompanied by some new limi-
tation.

But for my grandmother herself, the disease had almost
seemed liberating. For the first time in all the years I'd known
her, JoAnn appeared truly happy. She smiled all the time.
Over and over, she repeated, "Isn't everything beautiful!" or
"Ain't she sweet?" or simply, "Sooo nice." At first, this new
happiness struck me as feeble and pitiable, another awful reminder of her diminished mental capacity. But those weeks
with Yvella showed me how naïve I'd been. By the time my
mother-in-law was finally discharged from the hospital and
I escorted her back to her overlarge, too expensive house, I
did so with the conviction that real tragedy involves watching someone you love suffer, and not being able to alleviate
that suffering. It involves helplessly observing a loved one's
unhappiness, not their happiness. And that the only grown-
up, mature response to JoAnn's peace and joy, her freedom
from pain and worry, was—regardless of its source—gratitude.

Imagine: to be freed from your memory. To have every
awful thing that ever happened to you wiped away. And not
just your past, but your worries about the future, too. Because
with no sense of time or memory, past and future cease to exist, along with all sense of loss and regret. Not to mention
grudges and hurt feelings, arguments and embarrassments.

I mean, my life has been a charmed one—chock-full of true
love and friendship and happiness and achievement. I consider myself an uncommonly blessed person. But I also grew
up the biggest sissy in a backwater, redneck Texas town well
before school districts were successfully sued for tolerating

bullying. Trust me, there were some unpleasant moments. The older I get, the more boring those moments seem—really just the typical tortures of any atypical American childhood. I'm over it, and in general, I think that without facing some kind of adversity, it's difficult to appreciate anything in life. However, there are times—when entering a gym locker room or a public restroom or even just a crowded reception hall—when a cold, stiff wave of terror and shame overcomes me, when a particularly harrowing memory flashes through my skull like a migraine headache, and it takes me a slow, country minute to remember who I am, and count my many blessings, count them one by one. When this happens, I get so pissed off with myself for allowing myself to be bothered by something so pointless and far-off. "I wish I could be smart enough to forget that" is the thought that inevitably passes through my mind. "I wish I could just wipe that right out of my mind and enjoy my lovely, lucky life."

That's the fantasy, isn't it? To have your record cleared. To be able not to merely forget, but to expunge your unhappy childhood or unrequited love or rocky marriage from your memory. To start over again.

There had always been an element of existential fury to my grandmother's barbed-wire wit, concerning her lost time and missed chances. But as her Alzheimer's advanced, she forgot to be angry. She seemed healthier, too. Her pace quickened, her complexion brightened, her hair thickened. She had the look of a woman without a care in the world, and with my help and my grandfather's MasterCard, even her wardrobe improved. Meanwhile, I learned to stop trying to correct her mistaken recollections, and instead to take pleasure in the time I had with her. After all, what was there to correct?

Poetry almost never boasts a practical application; as important as it is, it's rarely useful. But when I was a teenager, traumatized by the changes puberty was realizing on my body, I used to recite lines from a poem by Anne Sexton to myself in front of the mirror: "Oh, darling," the poet writes to her eleven, almost-twelve-year-old child, "let your body in, let it tie you in, in comfort . . . there is nothing in your body that lies. All that is new is telling the truth."

"There is nothing in your body that lies," I used to tell my unrecognizable, manly reflection, my newly stubbled chin and rising Adam's apple. "All that is new is telling the truth," I'd console myself when my voice broke humiliatingly in class. "Let your body in, let it tie you in, in comfort," I'd say, tripping coltishly over my overgrown feet. During that tragic teenage time—when I was no oil painting, let me tell you—JoAnn accepted me with a grandmother's obvious, beaming pride. "Look at you," she'd say, eyeing me up and down. "Look at who you *are*! Who is this *man* of mine? Not a little boy anymore." She said this not as though she had lost any part of me, but as though she was honored to join me in the man I was becoming.

Now it was my turn. It was time for me to accept her own honest turning. It was my chance to be proud of JoAnn for the woman she was becoming.

Her change was the truth. It was a fact of nature, like puberty. What was gone in her was *not* missing, and to refuse to accept that would have been worse than illogical; it would have been cruel in a way that my grandmother never was to me.

"Nothing in her body lies," I reminded myself throughout 2005. And with time and experience, I learned—just as I had learned during my own adolescence—that this acceptance wasn't as sad and scary as it first appeared.

It seemed that everywhere I went with JoAnn—out to lunch or to the hairdresser's—people stopped me to say what a joy my grandmother was, what a pleasure it was to talk with such a "positive" person, or even how much they appreciated her advice! This advice, as I later discovered, was almost solely comprised of "Screw the bastards. You're beautiful!" Which, let's face it, does cover a multitude of sins.

Let me compare this to the counsel she'd offered a depressive young woman a couple of years earlier, who'd been brought to JoAnn's for tea by a well-meaning neighbor. "What's the matter with you?" JoAnn inquired. "Who comes over to somebody's house for a cup of tea and then just mopes around?" Which prompted the young woman to explain rather defensively that she'd just been fired from her job by a manager she was convinced was embezzling funds. "It's just not fair," she made the mistake of saying. "Fair!" JoAnn pounced, launching into a speech I knew well. "Fair! You know what's unfair? John F. Kennedy getting his brains blown out by some stoogey lunatic while his beautiful wife, who was dressed to perfection, by the way, crawls onto the back of a trunk! In Dallas, yet! Now that, sweetheart, is what you call 'not fair!'"

That's the kind of advice JoAnn used to give. The kind that made you wish you'd never been born—advice that might have stressed how beautiful Jackie Kennedy was, but never, ever you.

But now, Rena—a goddess with a master's degree who'd consented, for reasons that will never be clear to me, to help my grandparents out around the house—told me that the finest part of her day was her morning chat with my grandmother. JoAnn's transformation began to seem magical and unmistakable. She'd become a Southern Madwoman of Chaillot. To borrow her own logic, her Alzheimer's was definitely not fair, but it was reality, and, I was beginning to feel, not an altogether tragic one. Certainly not compared to the Kennedy assassination. And certainly not compared to Yvella's predicament. From this perspective, it seemed insane to squander all my sympathy on my grandmother, so safe and surrounded by friends and love and happiness.

SIX

The Living End

By the fall of 2006, JoAnn was talking to the teapot. She was flirting with the scarecrows she'd seated around the dining room, bickering with billboards, winking at her shoe, and otherwise relishing the fruits of having gone quite merrily insane.

The more that JoAnn forgot, the more she reminded me of *Harvey*'s Elwood P. Dowd, who says, "In this world, you must be oh so smart, or oh so pleasant. For years I was smart. I recommend pleasant." Only JoAnn didn't stop at pleasant. She rode straight on to giddy, with a song in her heart. And not just her heart. Something no doctor will ever be able to explain to me is how JoAnn, who often forgot who Alfred and I were, never forgot who Judy Garland was. I mean, it was astounding, really. She couldn't for the life of her recall that she lived in Tennessee, but she knew the whole of *Oklahoma!*, and quite a lot of *Carousel*. With infuriating irony, JoAnn *did* remember "the way you wear your hat, the way you sip your tea"—the memory of all that, as it turned out, being something they really couldn't take away from her, even though she drove the household batty with her unremitting cheerful chirping.

Having never been a particularly peppy person—having, in fact, been somewhat firmly antipep—JoAnn was suddenly up with a burst at sunrise and dressed before a hearty breakfast. And then, again after breakfast. And then, before lunch, and then after lunch—sometimes changing her clothes a dozen times a day. Or not changing them, but adding one dress on top of the next, scarf over scarf, hat atop hat, with two unmatched shoes, until she'd bundled herself like a very chic Eskimo, and, with difficulty, waddled downstairs.

For years, JoAnn had been treated for lupus—another disease, like Alzheimer's, notoriously elusive to diagnosis and testing. Suddenly, all signs of lupus stopped appearing in her blood work. "Your grandmother has Alzheimer's, right?" her doctor asked me.

I glanced at JoAnn, chewing on her zipper. "Yes, that's right," I answered.

"Well," said the doctor, shrugging. "There is a theory that people with Alzheimer's cure themselves of diseases because they don't know they have them."

It's an idea that particularly appeals to me, since I prefer story to science and tend to hear the fairy tale in everything. But then, Alzheimer's has its fairy-tale touches, doesn't it? There are parts of it that resemble those stories where a beautiful lady lives under a spell in a dark wood, a lady who loses her life or her looks or her identity before everything is magically restored to her in the last couple of pages.

Even still, I was not without my apprehensions, on that bracing blue September day before my birthday, as my grandparents and I swerved perilously through the Tennessee hills in their long white Buick to fetch Mother from the Nashville airport. Though I'd remained convinced that JoAnn's Remarkable Transformation couldn't fail to soften Mother's daughterly heart, it suddenly occurred to me that it was distinctly possible that the next several days might turn out . . . differently. In fact, it only now struck me that they *might* really suck. I have a friend named Agatha back in New York City who happens to be right about practically everything, and who'd all but predicted disaster before I left town.

"You say your mother and grandmother have always hated each other?" Agatha asked me, just before I caught a cab to the airport to fly to Nashville.

"That's right," I said.

"And they haven't been able to sit in the same room together for the past twenty years?"

"Give or take," I said.

"And your grandparents live far out in the country? In total isolation? With no close neighbors? No nearby diversions or entertainments?"

"Something like that."

"And you'll all be out there for a week? Totally alone?"

"Oh, yes, absolutely alone."

"Well, that does sound promising," she said, with one eyebrow noticeably higher than the other. "Call me the moment you get back."

At the time, I'd dismissed this warning as anxious fretting, and if anything, it had only stiffened my spine to soldier on, trusting to Providence. But now that I reconsidered the situation—during that risky, rocky drive to the airport to pick up Mother—it did seem somewhat possible that she would fail to notice any change in JoAnn at all. Perhaps that sounds unlikely, given JoAnn's condition. Mother can, after all, be a keenly perceptive woman when she wants to be. But brother,

only when she wants to be. Because when it conveniences her
to ignore established fact or to choose her own pretty fantasies over the truth, she's capable of maintaining a near-
impenetrable elective blindness. Look how long it took her to
cast a cold eye over Peter Ickpudth! Just because he happened
to bear a passing resemblance to Fess Parker!

Then again, I suppose it's not entirely fair to hold a person
like Mother, who really can be visionary when it comes to applying her makeup or styling a wig, to any rigorous standard
of reality. I mean, the woman's approach to eye shadow alone
is positively revelatory, and it's been my experience that
people who possess that kind of abstract creative ability can't
ever be forced to hold their hand to the plow, as it were. In
other words, I grew increasingly aware, as Alfred careened the
car around a few particularly dicey curves, that it was entirely
feasible that Mother would take one good look at JoAnn,
bounding after invisible butterflies like a golden retriever, or
shooting the breeze with Big Aunt Lela, who died in 1957, and
say, "Alzheimer's. What Alzheimer's?"

Just as it was conceivable that JoAnn, upon meeting her
daughter again, would experience one of her rare, inconve-
niently timed moments of lucidity and spoil the whole damn
thing by saying something just awful like, "I wish I'd never
bought you that Jody Wig." Such moments occurred now and
then, as unpredictable as summer rain. Like one morning the
previous June, when my grandparents' ancient, sputtering air
conditioner was once again on the fritz, and I was straining to
make up JoAnn's bed just the way I knew she liked it, and she
looked me straight in the eye and said, "You. Are. FAT. And.
You. Are. SWEATY." All with that fangy, cigarette-swishing
kind of Bette Davis diction, so that every word released a tiny

dose of venom into my bloodstream. My reaction to out-
bursts like this was always mixed. I knew that it wasn't really
JoAnn talking when lousy comments like this came slither-
ing out of her mouth. But on the other hand, I sometimes
experienced the faintest twinge of nostalgia on those now-
rare occasions when my grandmother managed to say something biting, and was tempted to run into her arms crying,
"JoAnn! You've come back to me!"

Mother, however, could not be expected to react similarly.
She had long ago given up hope of breaking through to JoAnn,
and so, I feared, my grandmother's Alzheimer's would, in some
sense, be irrelevant. But to an extent that seemed to threaten
my own happiness, I found that I'd poured all my prayers into
the hope that these two women I loved so profoundly could
find a way of loving each other—or at least stop fighting—that
we could, finally, be a family. That probably sounds schmaltzy
or selfless, and I'm usually neither. It's just that with JoAnn
fading so fast, I felt I was working under a very emphatic
deadline. As much as I tried not to overemphasize the importance of this meeting and to present this week as a light-
hearted little birthday celebration, it was almost certainly our
last chance to start over again, at least during JoAnn's lifetime.

All I could hope for, in the scheme of things, was a sort of
eleventh-hour reprieve from the governor. As a writer, I was
well aware that, to a large extent, a story is happy or sad because of the way it ends. Like the song says, "It's not where
you start, it's where you finish." It's whether the boy ends
up getting the girl, and whether the innocent goes free, and
whether the young dreamer finds success in the big, dark city.
All you need is a powerhouse finale, and nobody cares what

happened before. And that's what I was praying for as my grandparents' Buick rounded into the Nashville airport. Unlike when I was a child, I knew I couldn't force an outcome, push, or fool anybody to change their mind about anything. I was pretty sure that I couldn't hope to create an honorable end out of dishonorable means. All I could do was pray, "Lord in heaven, please give my family a happy ending."

Even in my state of heightened skepticism, I had to admit that our little reunion got off to a strong start as soon as we arrived at the airport. While JoAnn and Alfred waited in the car, I went looking for Mother at baggage claim and immediately spotted her sitting on top of her suitcases. It's never difficult to spot Mother and her suitcases. It's never difficult to spot Mother anywhere, really. There's something about the way she carries herself, with her big blond confidence, that sort of implies a spotlight. Sitting there, in the midst of the Nashville airport, perched atop her old Vuitton cases, with her legs crossed and an unlit cigarette clutched in her fingers, biding its time, it occurred to me that few passersby would have been surprised had she suddenly burst into "La Vie en Rose."

Something I've always noticed is the way a person's luggage can serve as a sort of stowable, packable Rorschach test, so that just by watching a suitcase glide slowly around a carousel, without ever seeing the person it belongs to, you can tell volumes about their taste and background. For instance, I think anybody observing my luggage would probably end up attributing the term "willy-nilly" or the phrase "flying by the seat of his pants" to my character. That's because my luggage tends less toward actual suitcases and more toward the kind of plastic duffel bags that are suggestive of homelessness or, at best, an extremely wayfaring personality. Whereas

Mother's fancy French luggage suggests an entirely different standard of living. She travels with the kind of hard-backed suitcases that went out of style with porters and bellhops. They're miniature steamer trunks, really, straight out of a forties movie. That's perfect for Mother because she's straight out of a forties movie, too—a big-shouldered, chain-smoking broad in towering heels, all worldly-wise and glamorous.

When I spotted Mother, she was already projecting a palpable sense of foreboding. On that Indian summer morning, Mother looked cool in a cream linen pantsuit. Fat gold jewelry dripped off her like ripened fruit. She looked ferocious, as usual, but also a little edgy. I called out to her, and after kissing both my cheeks Mother took my face in her hands and said, "I am not looking forward to this."

"It's going to be fabulous," I assured her. "Things have changed."

"We'll see," said Mother archly. "Any plans for the week? I mean, besides the mother-and-child reunion?"

"JoAnn and Alfred don't get out much anymore."

"I see. What about tomorrow night? Your birthday? What's the big plan for that?"

"We're just sticking around the house, really."

"Alone?"

"Alone."

"Just the four of us. Totally isolated, way out in the country."

"Well, we're really not that far from town. Not if you take the shortcut, anyway."

"The shortcut, Robert?"

"Yes," I stammered, "there's a . . . shortcut. Back to town."

Mother patted me on the back. "Happy birthday, Robert,"

she said. "In case I forget to tell you later. Happy, happy birthday."

Mother and I lugged her luggage out into the shining September morning and found JoAnn and Alfred standing beside the car, holding hands like teenage lovers. JoAnn smiled into the middle distance, but Alfred stared anxiously our way. "Well," Mother said to me, taking a deep breath, "we who are about to die salute you."

"Look, Annie," said Alfred, pointing toward us. "Look who it is. That's Jessica."

JoAnn focused her gaze upon Mother. "Isn't that funny," she said. "I have a daughter named Jessica." Then, all at once, like a cat pouncing on a ball of string, JoAnn leaped forward and embraced Mother. Her arms enwrapped her daughter entirely, squeezing her into a wad of cream linen. "Hello, you!" JoAnn softly screamed.

Mother forced a smile and attempted to gracefully wriggle out of JoAnn's anaconda grasp. "Oh, my. Goodness. Well, isn't that a nice, tight greeting. Hello . . . you." She patted down the creases in her suit and, still looking down, said, "Hello, Daddy."

"Jessica," he said. His plump little body bounced clumsily toward her. "I'm so . . . well . . . pleased . . . that you could make it. I hope you're . . . pleased . . . to be here. Your mother and I are just very . . . pleased . . . you could come."

"Well, I wouldn't have missed Robert's birthday for the world. He and I have always been very close. As you know, I've always had a wonderful relationship with my child."

"My, it's warm today," I piped in. "Why don't we all pile into the car and get that air conditioner cranked up? And I'll find some way to get this luggage into the trunk."

"Yes, yes," my grandfather grunted. "Good man. Good man."

Mother shot me a wary look, but she softened visibly once she climbed into the backseat of the Buick and my grandmother reached for her hand. "Tell me all about yourself, darlin'," JoAnn said. "I want to know everything about you."

"I beg your pardon," said Mother. JoAnn looked confused.

"She means it," I whispered from the front passenger seat. "Tell her something about yourself."

Mother made that horsey sound with her lips, when you exhale a gust of air with your mouth closed. "Well," she said. "I don't quite know where . . ."

"You're from Texas," I volunteered.

"Yeah, sure," said Mother. "I'm from Texas."

"I'm from Texas, too!" JoAnn said excitedly.

"I had a feeling," said Mother.

"And you love the movies," I said.

"Uh-huh." Mother nodded. "I love the movies."

"Ohhhh," JoAnn moaned, closing her eyes as though savoring something delicious and leaning her head back. "Don't you just?" She clutched Mother's hand to her chest. "Love the movies, I mean. I know I do. I just love them so."

Mother looked as though she were testing her weight on a rotten board, stepping tentatively, deeply uncertain as to how to proceed. "Well, so do I," she said finally.

"We have so much in common," JoAnn enthused.

"More than you might imagine," said Mother.

"Somehow I just knew we would. Didn't you? Didn't you just *know*?"

All the way back to the house, JoAnn carried on with bald affection, cuddling up to her daughter like a warm puppy, while Mother seemed of two minds: as if she wanted to jump out of the car onto the freeway, and also as if she wanted to climb into her mother's lap. I tried to play it casual. I tried not to stare too openly at the seduction taking place in the backseat, but the strangeness of the sight was remarkable: my mother trying hard to resist the charms of her mother, the person in all her life from whom she'd most wanted love.

Alfred and I made a good Texas dinner that evening, meaning red meat and red wine and a thick double-chocolate cake. Mother barely ate a bite, and she didn't touch a drop of the wine, either. Even if she hadn't been sober, she wouldn't have needed to drink to make it through that dinner. She was already intoxicated by JoAnn's attentions. JoAnn's "fascination" might have been generally dimmed by illness, but on that evening, she shone. It was as though her light was refracted through Alzheimer's, blazing through the cracks of her infirmity. That night, JoAnn might have forgotten the information of her life, her biographical data, but she seemed to remember who she *was*. From her thronelike chair, she aimed all her star quality, all her twinkling, undulating charm, directly at my mother. She beamed and petted and doted upon her daughter, my mother, who seemed flustered and ruffled, thrown off balance by her mother's courtship.

Later that evening, Mother made a grand theatrical production of rooting through the closet in her bedroom.

"What *are* you doing?" I asked.

"Looking for space pods," she answered furiously. "Who are those people, Robert? And what have they done with my mother? I keep thinking I must be in a blackout." Mother flung herself onto the bed. "I keep thinking I must be drunk in a ditch somewhere, and when I wake up, I'm going to have the hangover of a lifetime. Because believe you me, if that nice old lady had been my mother, I'd never have left home."

"And now, that nice old lady is your mother."

"I'm still not convinced," Mother said, staring up at the ceiling. "I think some sort of trickery is afoot. I think you've somehow managed to forge her, like you did my handwriting that time you wrote her that terrible letter when you were twelve years old."

"You're being ridiculous." I sat at the foot of Mother's bed. "And Alfred, too. He's been very sweet."

"Yeah, he's all right. But it was never really him I had the problem with. He was always just a sort of winged-monkey figure. She was the evil one."

"*Evil*, Mother?"

"*Christmas was lost for the want of a Jody Wig.*"

"Oh, brother."

"Don't you *oh, brother* me," Mother said. She propped herself up on her elbows. "You don't know. You don't know what it was like to grow up with the two of them. With a mother and father who didn't give a shit about me. You've been absolutely worshipped since the day you were born, and I've got the home movies to prove it. So don't you *oh, brother* me, Robert."

"You're right," I said. "I'm sorry. I don't know what it was like."

"You sure as hell don't."

"But it's different now."

"Yeah, because she's a bedbug."

"She's not a bedbug, Mother."

"Pretty damn close. That's what it took for my mother to be sweet to me. She had to lose her cotton-pickin' mind."

"But I was right. Things have changed."

"They've changed all right." She flung herself back down on the bed.

"And there is an opportunity here. Now. You do have an opportunity with your mother that never existed before. You could have everything you ever wanted from your parents."

"I still can't talk to her. It's not like we can have a conversation or anything."

"Why can't you talk to her? Go ahead, talk to her."

"About what?"

"How the hell should I know? Anything you want."

"It isn't as though she'd be able to respond."

"She'll respond. I don't know how. But she'll respond . . . in some way. Besides, it isn't as though healthy parents ever respond the way you want them to, anyway."

"Wait a—"

"That wasn't a dig, I promise. But go ahead. When was the last time you knew what your future held? So go ahead. First thing tomorrow morning, pour out your girlish heart to your old mama."

"Robert, I'm fifty-three years old. It's a little late in the day."

"Look, I'm not saying you have to be the Waltons."

"Oh, we *don't* have to be *the Waltons*? Jesus, that sheds another light on the situation entirely."

"All I'm saying is, you've gone through your whole life as a person whose mother never loved her. You've gone through your whole life as a person who didn't love her mother. And this could be an opportunity to be free from all that. You could be a woman whose mother is a sweet old lady."

"A sweet old lady who's a bedbug."

"Mother, don't. She's sick. It isn't nice."

"I'll call her any damn thing I . . . Bedbug, bedbug, bed-bug."

"Very mature."

She sprang up onto her elbows again. "Don't you tell me about—"

"Look, you're sober, right?" I interrupted.

"Today, I'm sober."

"Well, does it matter how long it took you to get sober? Isn't late better than never?"

"That's what I'm trying to determine. It would seem as though late is better than never. But then, some things . . ." She trailed off sadly. "For some things there's a planting season. That's all I'm saying."

"For some things," I said. "But not for loving your mother. Or at least for not hating her."

"Jesus," Mother said. "We've had one good dinner. That's all. Who knows if the weather will hold."

"I believe it will."

"I love you," said Mother. "I love you. Sweet dreams. Good night."

"You're kicking me out?"

"I need rest. Beauty sleep. I need to set tomorrow's wig and collect my thoughts. I have a lot to try to make sense of. Jesus, a vodka tonic would taste good right about now. Go to bed, go to bed, go to bed."

"I love you, Mother," I said.

"I know you do," she said. "And it's to my ever-lovin' credit that you know what that means. And that you take it for granted that I love you. Which I do, with all my heart. Now, scram. Skedaddle. Good night."

That whole week, the weather held. The starchy blue

autumn skies remained clear, and so did the irony. Now that my grandmother had, in a sense, disappeared, she was fully present to my mother for perhaps the first time in their relationship. Now that she was all but unreachable, she was finally available.

"How *are* you, sweetheart?" JoAnn asked Mother over lunch on the back patio a couple of days later. I'd made tuna salad and sun tea. Mother was very meticulously removing the capers from her tuna salad with her iced-tea spoon, making a tiny little pile of them on her bread plate. On the lawn, the sun was broiling, but on the patio, it was pleasant and cool, another season entirely.

"I loathe capers," Mother said. "They don't contribute anything to tuna. They're the interlopers of a perfectly respectable salad."

"No," said JoAnn, leaning toward Mother. "I mean, how *are* you?"

"Besides the capers, I'm fine."

"Mother," I sighed.

"Oh, what, Robert. What? What do you want me to say? What do either of you want me to say?"

"Something more personal than tuna," I said.

JoAnn stared keenly into her daughter's face.

"Fine," said Mother. "I'm sober, so that sucks, but at least it means that I probably won't have to pick up any more garbage on the side of the freeway. So there's a plus. But on the downside, I'm starting to realize how much of the rest of my life sucks. My husband is an asshole who's had to perform even more community service than I have and occasionally tries to beat the shit out of me."

"Do I know him?" asked JoAnn. "If I know him, I'll kill him."

"No, you knew the first one, who left me for a pregnant jockey. I'm on my second terrible marriage. I hate my life. I hate Northern California. I hate the fucking ocean and all the fucking hippies, with all their sad fucking ponytails and paella and pesto and macrobiotic Whole Foods, woodsy bullshit. I'll be sixty in, like, five minutes. I'm totally friendless. I'm going to need another face-lift by, say, Tuesday. I'm destined for yet another divorce. And I still don't know what I want to be when I grow up. And I fucking hate fucking fucking capers," Mother said, picking up her bread plate and Frisbee-tossing it off the patio. "So that's how I fucking am. Okay, JoAnn? Okay, Robert?" She slammed her hands down on the table, and for a moment I sat listening to the ice cubes clacking around the tea glasses.

"Well, fucking okay," JoAnn said merrily. "Okay," she said, picking up her bread plate, and tossing it onto the lawn. "Go ahead," she said, turning to me. "Go ahead. What are you waiting for?"

"Well, okay," I said, throwing my plate gamely after theirs.

"*Fucking* okay," said JoAnn. "Whoever wanted capers in the first place? Fuck it."

The following morning, while my mother was still upstairs sleeping, my grandmother found me reading at the breakfast table.

"Robert," she said. She rushed furtively to my side, hovering over me like a moth in a peignoir. "Robert, Alfred just told me that Jessica's my *daughter.*" She seemed perfectly astounded.

"That's right," I said. "Isn't that marvelous?"

"But don't you think that's extraordinary? Can you believe that nobody *ever* told me that before?"

"Maybe they just wanted to surprise you."

"But Robert," she said, sitting beside me. "I've been thinking it over. And I realized that I haven't seen Jessica, I mean really *seen* her, in, God, maybe thirty years. And then, I started thinking, 'What kind of a mother doesn't see her own daughter for thirty years?' The thing of it is, I always thought of myself as a good mother. I mean, I always thought that even if I'd had an ugly little baby, I'd have done whatever it is you *can* do for an ugly baby. But now I realize that's not true. And it just kills me. I mean, I sure never thought I was the kind of woman who'd spend her whole life not seeing her only daughter," she said. "And God, how do you start doing something about that?"

"Tell her," I said, suppressing the desperation in my voice. "Oh, why don't you just tell her that?" I knew, from many a margarita-fueled night, that it was precisely what my mother had waited most of her life to hear.

JoAnn widened her eyes and gave a little cough. "Well, of course I will, if there's time," she said, offended. "But, Robert, there's something else. If Jessica's my daughter, that has to mean that *you're* my grandson."

"Absolutely," I said.

"Well, that's *so* wonderful," she said. "I mean, hell, I knew that I liked you. I knew you were always hanging around here. But nobody ever told me we were blood. Isn't that just the living end?"

"It *is* the living end," I said, trying hard to keep my voice from cracking. "Though there is," I said, "a downside."

"What?" JoAnn eyed me suspiciously.

"You and I can never have sex."

"Well, Jesus Christ," she said, rising quickly. She gripped the collar of her peignoir to her throat. "I knew you'd say *something* to fuck it all up!" Then JoAnn smiled at me and patted her collar back down. "The living end . . ." I heard her muttering as she left the kitchen.

In the meantime, my mother seemed perfectly astounded by the change in JoAnn. Throughout that week, Mother's native bravado began to fall away. She seemed to be melting before my very eyes. She looked younger and more vulnerable, like a little girl who's lost her mother in the supermarket. Each evening, as JoAnn scooted closer at dinner, my mother seemed to find her nearness less nerve-racking.

On the last day of our trip, as were leaving for the airport, my grandfather kissed us good-bye. Soft black cows strode serenely on the hillside. Suddenly, JoAnn grabbed the lapels of my mother's jacket, as if she were about to shake her. "Thank you for coming, Jessica. I want you to know how much it means to me. I want you to know that *I* know we've never been close. And I know that's been mostly my fault. I'm not sure how much time I've got. But more than anything, I want to have a shot at spending it with you. It's so important. I mean, after all, Jessica, we're *sisters*."

I groaned, then looked over to see my tough mother crying.

"Close enough, Mama," she said. "Close enough."

SEVEN

Twelve Miles of Bad Road

In the two years following her stroke, Yvella Leleux had only continued to fade, but with a slowness that made it all but impossible to see, as though she'd gone for a stroll on a late spring evening convinced that the purple light would hold and found herself lost in a dark that was not quite night, but also not quite day. Michael and I talked to her on the phone constantly and flew back to Houston as often as we could. For the first six months after her long stay in the hospital, she seemed buoyed by a business scheme that Michael hatched for her, of buying and selling antique china online. Michael's plan *did*, at first, seem to have the makings of an ideal cottage industry. Mom could buy fairly priced sets of china on eBay, then resell them piece by piece at a small profit, all from the comfort of her home. But then the scheme hit an insurmountable snag.

Mom accomplished the first, developmental stage of her business plan with aplomb: She had absolutely no trouble buying china on eBay. In fact, in no time at all, she exhibited a really splendid facility for buying any variety of items on the Internet. It was, alas, the second stage of Michael's business plan, that all-important (at least in the profit-making sense) selling stage that seemed to befuddle her. For, despite the ease and fluency with which she purchased, Mom suffered a crippling mental block about selling. So crippling, in fact, that she never sold a single thing. And so, by late summer 2006, before any of us realized quite what was happening, her "business" morphed horribly into a galloping online shopping addiction.

Suddenly Mom went from bidding on antique porcelain to staying up all night buying worthless, creepy junk in terrifying quantities. Maybe "creepy" sounds like the wrong adjective to attribute to online auction finds, but what would you call the sudden appearance, in your sweet old Catholic mother-in-law's parlor, of several dozen white patent leather jazz shoes with pink georgette silk laces in assorted men's sizes? Next to twenty-odd plaster mannequin heads? And a hundred or so of those velvet fingers they use to display rings in jewelry stores? Which, when they're all laid out side by side, give the impression of scores of people behaving very rudely toward one another?

Then Mom branched out and started bidding on something called "auction lots," which is sort of the Vegas version of online shopping where nobody tells you precisely what you're bidding on. They only provide you with a general description of the kind of items contained within the lot. And *that,* incredibly, is meant to be the appeal of bidding on auction lots—the idea that some random cardboard box you're blindly throwing money after could end up being a veritable Aladdin's cave, filled with veiled, unconjured treasure instead of some pile of disgusting crap that nobody in their right mind would ever want in the first place, like grimy café curtains and miniature porcelain toilet bowls and filthy old baby clothes. Old baby clothes! Mom bought box after cardboard box stuffed with old baby clothes! You know that short story by Hemingway that everybody thinks is so fabulous because it's only six words long? The one that goes: "For Sale. Baby shoes. Never worn." Well, if Yvella Leleux had ever spotted those words on eBay, she wouldn't have thought "literary masterpiece"; she would have thought "bargain shopping," and she would have right-clicked "Buy now" as fast as her little mouse allowed her. In no time at all, it seemed that some kind of techno-fueled Plague of Egypt had befallen Mom's parlor, causing boxes to gather and swarm like locusts up to the ceiling, overflowing into the front hallway, the family and dining rooms.

In retrospect, it's difficult to remember precisely when Mom stopped looking like a budding Mrs. Fields, and started looking more like Ray Milland in *The Lost Weekend*. But it was probably somewhere around the time she decided to give away all her living room furniture so that she could mount clothing racks to the downstairs walls, with the aim of turning her house—in the midst of a rigorously deed-restricted neighborhood, mind you—into a sort of suburban resale shop.

I say that Mom decided upon this plan of action, but I don't mean to imply that she informed Michael or me of it. Instead, she told our teenage nephew, who was then trying to furnish a stag pad in his garage, so that by the time we were made aware of Mom's intentions, her sofa was already on the back of a truck, and Michael had to spend a whole Saturday afternoon negotiating its return.

For me, this was a red flag. But it wasn't for Michael, who refused to admit that there was anything at all unusual about turning your house into a Salvation Army. "She's just exploring some new marketing options," Michael assured me. "She's experienced a few bumps in the road. A few rocky patches. But now she's feeling her way through various new retail strategies."

"Are you listening to yourself?" I asked him. "Can you actually hear yourself talking right now? You sound like one of those slimy Wall Street lawyers explaining what their ex-C.E.O. clients are going to do after they get out of prison. Your mother is not exploring marketing strategies, Michael. She's giving away every valuable thing she owns so that she can open a mannequin-head, café-curtain, miniature toilet-bowl boutique in what used to be her living room. Does this sound like rational behavior to you?"

"Look, Robert," Michael sighed wearily. "She's been through a really hard time. I just don't want to discourage her in the first thing she's been excited about in ages. Let's just give her a little latitude here, okay?"

"You mean, give her enough rope to hang herself," is what I said to myself. But "Fine" is what I actually said. "She's your mother. Heaven knows I've got mothers of my own."

A few weeks later, we awoke to discover that Mom had run through her scant savings and was thousands of dollars overdrawn in her checking account, having grossly miscalculated the cost, with shipping, of her latest round of manic, middle-of-the-night eBay buys. At which time even Michael was forced to admit that his mother had a problem. By then, however, the die had been cast, because when Yvella found herself unable to pay up, eBay shuttered her account with a resounding thud, and with that, the expensive, misguided, fragile bubble of hope that had sustained Mom suddenly burst and settled into a puddle of despair.

It took months for us to understand what was happening, but after that, Mom sounded a little sadder each time we spoke to her, a tad more convinced that she'd outlived her usefulness. She lived in an atmosphere of defeat. Her home, once so sunny and bustling, grew darkened by dusty piles of unopened cardboard boxes that obscured doors and windows. Piles of baby clothes covered the floor. Attempts at organizing the mess were frustrated by Mom's uncertainty as to what she wanted to do with it all. She seemed resistant to parting with any of her insanely gotten goods, relating to them as a form of frozen capital. This accumulation of stuff accompanied a general decline in the life of the house. Shingles rotted and went unreplaced. Appliances broke and went unrepaired. The house was like a woman who manages through the years to retain a slim and youthful figure, a taut and lineless visage, until all at once, in the course of a single year, time overtakes her and accomplishes all of its cruel work in one brief spell. With Mom's sadness, the house lost its life and vitality and suddenly seemed a forlorn place.

"It's all so tragic," I told Mother over the telephone around that time. "Michael's family's house looks like Grey Gardens."

"Yeah," she said, "except nobody's a Kennedy."

"Thank you, Mother," I said. "Very compassionate, I'm sure. Very Christian of you."

"I mean, *no*body's a Kennedy. Not any of 'em."

"I got it," I said, "no one's a Kennedy. That's indisputable, yes."

"I mean not a single last cotton-pickin' one of 'em's a Kennedy. There's not a Eunice. There's not a Joe. There's not a Joan or a Sargent or a Rosemary—"

"Lovely. That's lovely of you, Mother. Always a tender shoulder. I'm hanging up now. Love you bunches. Good-bye."

In summer 2007, Mom finally announced her intention of putting the house up for sale in an attempt to take charge of her finances. This was, in and of itself, a good idea—just what we'd hoped for, actually. In fact, most of her children and sons-in-law had silently prayed for the day she'd decide to slough off that huge house and its crippling mortgage. We'd all opened our homes to her, offering comfortable retirement options from East Coast to West. Michael and I, of course, wanted her to live with us in New York. But Mom eighty-sixed that notion right off the bat—not because of the traffic or noise or hustle-bustle of the Big Apple, but because she felt that Michael and I have too many houseguests. "I don't want strangers seeing me in my housecoat before my morning coffee," she said.

So instead, she declared her intention of moving into one of the saddest apartment buildings in East Texas, the sort of neo-Dickensian, core-doored nightmare frequently to be seen on *Cops*. It had "End of the Road" written all over it and its sole point of advantage, even according to Mom, was that it was located across the street from the hospital: "That way, I won't have to drive to the doctor anymore," Mom explained meekly. "And if things get too bad, they can always just wheel me on over." It seemed that Mom had reached a point where she didn't care if she was ever wheeled out again.

We all hoped to persuade Yvella not to take this disheartening step, but in order to make any change in her life, something had to be done about the house. Michael and his sisters decided its rehabilitation required a grand push, a group effort, before placing it on the market. After it was successfully listed with a real estate agent, Mom could be sent on an extended vacation to visit her daughter in the Midwest until it sold, at which time her new living arrangements could be determined. So that August, we all descended on Houston to spend a fetid, sizzling week cleaning out not only Yvella's eBay inventory, but also thirty years of Michael's family's life, its remainders and mementos and evidences. Unless you've undertaken a similar project, it's difficult to convey just how much stuff can accrue in a family house, even when that house hasn't become a storage bin for an insomniac's eBay compulsion. Aside from the towering piles of velvet fingers and such, the house was packed to the gills with eight-tracks and yearbooks, school essays and old linens, cooking utensils and abandoned art projects. It's also difficult to convey just what a heartrending trial it can be to decide the fate of each precious piece of your family's over-sentimentalized stuff. After all, who has the heart to throw away, even after thirty years, a child's Sunday school finger painting? A kindergartener's macaroni sculpture? Or the few surviving dishes of your parents' first set of dime store china? It takes a great steeling of the spirit to dispose of things like that. And ordinarily, it takes a lot of time. Time to decide what's valuable enough to keep, but also time to honor the past through reminiscing.

In my experience at least, there seems to be something about telling the stories of one's possessions that grants a person the freedom to give them away. Somehow, it allows you to hold on to your past without holding on to your objects, because passing on your stories is another way of bequeathing your heirlooms. It's a way of completing the past and moving on. Or at least, that's the conclusion I'd come to whenever I'd cleared out a closet or garage with my grandparents or with Mom. You know that mean joke people tell about desperate celebrities—that they'll attend the opening of a drawer? Well, in the past, it had actually been quite fascinating to open drawers with Mom and empty out their contents. She couldn't clean out a cabinet without launching into reverie, like when she told me the story of an ordinary white ceramic bowl she'd played with as a girl because her parents couldn't afford to buy her a doll. She and her sister Ruby had named the bowl Mrs. Montgomery, and when Ruby left home to get married, she gave Mrs. Montgomery to Mom, who had kept her ever since.

"You mean they just played with a *bowl*?" Mother said later when I telephoned to tell her this.

"Yes, isn't that just the saddest thing you ever heard?" I said.

"Just two little girls carrying a bowl around all day pretending like it was a person named Mrs. Montgomery?"

"It was the Great Depression," I said.

"Well, it was *something*," Mother answered.

One of the reasons Mom and I formed such a fast friendship when I first joined her family is that I've always been a real sucker for listening to stories like this, and Mom's always been a real sucker for telling them. So, one of the most terrifying aspects of that stultifying August week in Houston was that Mom was so obviously beyond talking about the past—beyond caring what happened to her things and, so it seemed, to herself. Mainly, Yvella sat in a chair and stared blankly at the wall, passively giving away most of the things she owned and loved. As her daughters bickered over who got the end tables, she maintained an unsettling silence. Over the previous few years, Mom had grown a trifle deaf, so that most people (not me, because I'm a loudmouth) have to speak up in order for her to hear them without effort. It's generally less of a handicap than a minor inconvenience. But that week, Mom seemed stone-deaf, almost unreachable by our voices and the world around her; she'd respond to most direct questions by smiling absently and nodding. It was as though she found the sadness of her situation unbearable and simply turned herself off. It was a concept I understood in principle because sometimes, when I find myself talking to an especially unpleasant person, I take my glasses off so that I can't see his yakking face anymore, which I find makes it easier to put up with practically anybody. But Mom's behavior, assuming it was a chosen behavior, seemed more extreme, and it troubled me.

"What about Mrs. Montgomery, Mom?" I asked, trying to rouse her interest any way I could. "What do you want to do with Mrs. Montgomery?"

"I think it's time to let her go," Mom said, without even turning to look my way. Any other time, her behavior might have passed for indifference, but under the circumstances, it was all I could do to keep from crying. As tenderly as I could, I took Mrs. Montgomery, and I stuck her in the far back of a cabinet filled with necessities for Mom's squalid new apartment, where I knew she wouldn't be found by anyone else.

One morning that week, craving privacy and a better air-conditioning system, I'd snuck away to the neighborhood Barnes & Noble and bought a cheap paperback copy of Horton Foote's beautiful play *The Trip to Bountiful*. Reading that play during Coca-Cola breaks from cleaning and packing, and those brief moments in bed at night before I passed out from exhaustion, I had no trouble imagining Yvella as Carrie Watts, the lace-collared lady whose will to live is so closely tied to her Texas home: "When you've lived longer than your house or your family, maybe you've lived too long," Mrs. Watts says. "Or maybe it's just me. Maybe the need to belong to a house and a family and a town has gone from the rest of the world." As we busily swept all evidence of her life out of her house, I could see Mom mulling over the same questions, about whether the world still held a place for people who loved a place filled with the past.

At week's end, after finalizing arrangements with a Realtor, Mom allowed herself to be loaded, along with her oxygen tank and several small suitcases, into the back of her daughter's Cadillac, and driven away for a short visit to Indiana. She appeared slightly dazed and of uncertain footing, almost as though her eyes hadn't managed to adjust to the blazing Houston light after stepping out of the dark house. Before the car pulled out of the driveway, she squinted back across the lawn, through the white heat and sunshine, and barely even waved good-bye. A couple of days later, Michael and I flew back to New York, worn out by the suburbs and longing for the peace and quiet of the big city.

During the month she stayed in Indiana, Yvella wound down like a clock. Until, within a few weeks, she'd stopped talking almost entirely and sat staring into space, looking frightened and pitiful. When she began trembling uncontrollably, Michael's sister took her to the local emergency room. By that point, it wasn't just Mom's heart that gave her trouble; she had diabetes and was regularly on the verge of kidney failure, which meant that any considered medical opinion of her well-being required a whole host of doctors, a variety of expert opinions. She was checked into the hospital for examination, at which point Michael and I drove down from New York.

Aside from a couple of trips to visit the art museums of Chicago as a child, I'd seen nothing of the Midwest. After a lifetime spent in the wonderful, wild, cowboy energy of Texas and the throb and thrum of Manhattan, hushed Indiana seemed foreign. People are always resistant to this idea, but Texans and New Yorkers have a lot in common. In both places, personalities are bred for size and splash. Needless to say, size and splash aren't of top concern to your typical, tight-lipped Hoosier. Due to the open-ended length of our stay, Michael and I checked into a seedy Red Roof Inn next to a strip club not far from the hospital, and even that strip club appeared to be lit by paler neon than that of Texas or New York. Before leaving home, I'd bought a pair of red Converse sneakers at the Gap, and during the three weeks we spent in Indiana, perhaps a dozen people, total strangers mostly, approached me to exclaim, "You're wearing red shoes!" However, as foreign as Indiana may have seemed, the hospital and its staff were entirely familiar. That's one of the most comforting things about hospitals: They're like the embassies of a single nation. No matter where you go, in America at least, they tend to look alike, they are governed by remarkably similar sets of rules, and they are staffed by remarkably similar, identically uniformed people. And so it was a great relief, but no great surprise, that the hospital nurses and administrators who first took us to Mom were virtual doubles of those good Houston folks at Methodist Hospital with whom I'd lived while Mom recovered from her stroke two years earlier.

When I was a teenager, I asked JoAnn why Southerners are funny and, without hesitation, she said, "Because we lost the war." Which is hilarious, and who knows, maybe even true (although, by this logic, the Germans and the Russians should be the funniest people in the world), but it also revealed something basic about JoAnn and the rest of my family: our belief that humor is both the antidote to suffering and the necessary by-product of suffering. Paraphrasing Franklin Roosevelt's great line, JoAnn would tell me, "The only thing to fear is the thing you can't make funny."

I had, then, according to my grandmother's logic, much to fear when Michael and I were first shown to Mom's room in that Indiana hospital, because the way she looked that morning was the least funny thing I've ever seen. Mom was wearing her pajamas and a tatty red cardigan I'd bought her at Nordstrom years ago. She stared blankly into space, and she trembled. It was as though she were freezing cold, like a small dog fresh from the bath. Her whole body quaked, and it wasn't merely that she was quiet, as she had been in Houston; she seemed almost unable to speak. You could see the words form at the base of her throat, then slowly work their way up her neck, where they stuck in her trembling mouth, until several seconds later, she spat them out. It was an agonizing process that reminded me of that fairy tale about the good sister who, when she spoke, spat out pearls and diamonds, and the bad sister, who spat out lizards and toads. In the rare moments when Mom tried hard to speak, it took her forever to finally spit out "yes" or "no," all the while wringing a Kleenex in her hands. Watching Michael attempt to communicate with her—to discover what was wrong, what had happened to upset her so—was the most pitiable sight I've ever witnessed.

Mom just stared past him, petrified and shaking, with her mouth pursed and her fingers wringing, wringing, wringing that Kleenex to pulpy bits.

My first suspicion was that she'd had another stroke. Haunted by memories of JoAnn, I fully expected the legion of tests being performed by Mom's team of doctors to say exactly that. But it wasn't so simple. By this point, her body was like a classic car, constantly in need of special care and regular tune-ups. Her "numbers" (blood pressure, blood sugar, creatinine levels) were constantly, often wildly, off. But this, in the peril-ous reality of Mom's physicality, was what passed for normal. Still, none of the Indiana doctors could detect any evidence of a stroke or any other "event" that might have prompted her ter-rible change.

Nor could the hospital's psychiatrist, a kindly, quiet man who cleared us out of her room in order to conduct several probing conversations with Mom. In these, he addressed the terror she exhibited and found her to be fully aware but over-whelmed by a sense of doom. Finally, as Mom later told us, he sighed, and said, "Mrs. Leleux, why don't you, if you can, tell me what it is you'd like to have happen, and I'll see if I can help you."

"I want," she told him slowly, "my son to take me home. I want to go back to my own house."

At that point, I honestly think Michael and I would have agreed to anything that held even the faintest promise of re-viving Mom. So when that psychiatrist walked into the lobby to which he'd driven us and said, "She wants to go home," we jumped at the prospect. It was a tall order. Michael had al-ready missed nearly three weeks of work, and taking Mom back to Texas would, at the very least, require a week more. A month spent even in places like the Red Roof Inn costs a mint—far more, in fact, than I had available on any of my credit cards. So I telephoned Mother and explained Yvella's dire situation.

"So what do you need from me?" Mother asked.

"Money," I said. "I need you to wire me some cash so Michael and I can take Mom back to Texas."

"I see," said Mother. "So, as it turns out, *I* am the Kennedy."

"That's right, Mother," I said. "If it makes you happy, then *you* are the Kennedy."

"It'll be waiting for you at Western Union," Mother said. "Code word: *Jackie.*"

Aside from time and money, returning Mom to her home was a tall order because the house itself was already boxed up, locked up, and being shown to potential buyers.

But, at the first moment permitted by the hospital, Michael and I packed up the old oxygen tank, wheeled Mom to the car, and hit the road. We spent most of our drive back to Texas on the telephone, talking to Realtors and relatives, making frenzied arrangements for Yvella's return. She, however, though now speaking with more ease, spent the first day of our trip in near-total silence, staring wanly out the window with the same sad, bewildered expression haunting her face. But at least she wasn't trembling.

Fortunately, I managed to steer our trip through Nashville and to my grandparents' farm. One of the most marvelous things about Nashville is that it's nearly smack-dab in the center of America and, always seeming to be halfway between wherever you are and wherever you're going, it makes an ideal way station. The town's willingness always to *be there,* to offer rest and shelter no matter where you're roaming, is an extremely endearing municipal quality. And never have I been more obliged for Nashville's hospitality than when we arrived at JoAnn and Alfred's. I felt rode hard and put up wet from the sheer panic and pressures of the past several weeks.

When I pulled the car into their endless, cow-strewn drive, I was as exhausted as I've ever been. Yvella was the most vulnerable, Michael was the most anxiety-ridden, and my grandparents the most dear. It was as though three seekers on a quest had landed at an enchanted cottage in the woods, where the elves promptly set about mending them. During those past weeks, a kind of shell shock had settled over us. But from the moment we arrived, JoAnn and Alfred refused even to comprehend Yvella's despondency or the fact that she'd spoken a mere handful of sentences in the past couple of weeks. The atmosphere of comfort and happiness that reigned at their house simply wouldn't tolerate it, just as the desert would evaporate mist or a rainstorm extinguish a flame. "How would you like me to show you around the farm, Mrs. Leleux?" my grandfather asked, relishing his role as Southern squire. "Or perhaps you'd prefer a nice brisk walk in the garden?"

"Um, no," Mom managed to spit out. "No, thank you," she said, casting desperate glances in Michael's direction.

"Ah, Mrs. Leleux," said my grandmother, madly twirling a lock of her hair. "I remember her well. She always wore a hat." Then JoAnn tiptoed toward the armchair to which Yvella had adhered herself. "Perhaps this will make you feel better," she said in her most benevolent, Junior League voice, retrieving a fuchsia pump with a two-inch heel from the square black pocketbook she'd taken to carrying twenty-four hours a day and placing it gingerly into Yvella's palm.

"Yes," said Mom, who, from that moment on, began watching JoAnn very carefully out of the corner of her eye. "Well, thank you very much."

Yvella hadn't seen my grandmother since the Christmas before her Alzheimer's began to take its toll, and at that point had found her extremely intimidating. "I'd like to be her friend someday," Mom had then said pitifully. "But I'm sure she and I don't travel in the same circles." She'd said it with such embarrassment that I'd been ashamed that anyone so kind could possibly fear exclusion from my family. Of course, I'd kept her abreast of JoAnn's altered state, but there was no way to prepare her for the Mad Hatter's tea party under way at my grandparents' house.

Alfred cleared his throat. "Maybe Michael and I should make a run into town and bring back some supper," he suggested.

"Yes, sir," said Michael. "I think we'd all benefit from a takeout dinner."

"And a rented movie," Alfred offered gallantly.

While they went to town, I stayed home to keep an eye on Yvella and JoAnn. My grandparents had a new puppy—an incorrigible, fluffy white bichon frise named Precious that had quickly established herself as head of household. Precious had been the suggestion of my grandmother's neurologist, who'd offered my family a sage bit of advice: "Sometimes people with Alzheimer's," she'd told us, "particularly ladies from another generation who're accustomed to basing their self-worth on caretaking, can feel purposeless once they become the object of everyone else's care. It could perhaps bring comfort to your grandmother to feel responsible for something. A puppy, for instance."

This was, without question, the most useful advice offered

us throughout JoAnn's illness—a fact few would have doubted after seeing the way JoAnn brushed, pampered, and carried on lengthy conversations with her new best friend. Precious— Vanquisher of Domestic Tranquility, Ravisher of Persian Rugs, Scourge of Sofa Legs—seemed to be the only living creature capable of matching my grandmother's new amped-up energy level. That dog became her doll and her playmate, and a source of endless joy and irritation to the rest of us. JoAnn and Precious took to spending most of the day chasing each other through the house, laughing and larking about, and playing a modified version of fetch in which JoAnn threw a tennis ball for Precious but then also retrieved it for her. My grandmother had an almost palpable need to care for that dog—just as she obviously felt a need to care for Yvella.

So while Michael and Alfred went for dinner, I watched as Precious ran lightning-speed laps around Mom's chair, emitting piercing barks. Yvella closed her eyes, leaned her head back, and moaned. And JoAnn trotted briskly throughout the house, hunting for further restorative items for Yvella—a ratty, old ball gown, a busted umbrella, a ceramic elephant, and a brown paper sack stuffed with socks and old lipsticks, all of which she piled lovingly into my mother-in-law's lap. "Thank you. Thank you very much, JoAnn," Yvella managed to tell her, with—I couldn't help notice—greater ease than she'd spoken since before she left Houston.

Then JoAnn conducted a reconnaissance of the back patio in search of further healing agents for Yvella, like a wind chime and a potted geranium. The second she opened the back door, Precious staged a getaway. Such getaways were a fact of life with that dog, who managed to escape almost daily with one objective in mind—to herd the cattle in the front pasture and then wallow in the creek until her downy white fur was completely coated in mud. The sun was already starting to set. Unless I wanted to spend the better part of an hour wading after Precious through the muck, and then shampooing and blow-drying her back into a civilized state, I knew I had to head her off before she reached the creek. But that meant leaving Yvella and JoAnn alone for a few minutes. It was a gamble, and I went for it.

Apparently, I was barely out the door before Yvella spotted JoAnn dragging an eight-by-ten-foot knotted wool rug down the spiral staircase. And motivated by the same caretaking impulse that had made Precious such a superior (albeit frustrating) companion for my grandmother, Yvella bounded out of her armchair, believing JoAnn was about to take a tumble. "Now, you just put that heavy old thing down, darlin', before you hurt yourself," she said, seeing JoAnn sway like an aspen tree under the weight of the rug, toddling perilously from one step to the next. Yvella reached out for my grandmother's hand and, while trying gently to pry the rug away from her, Yvella lost her balance and started to fall backward. Attempting to save her, JoAnn dropped the rug and latched on to Mom's waist, causing both women to come crashing down to the floor, where I found them sitting a few minutes later, hugging each other and laughing their asses off.

"What happened?" I asked, trying to thwart Precious's efforts to squirm free from my arms.

JoAnn was breathless and panting with glee, but Yvella managed to howl, "I was trying . . . to help her . . . and then, we both fell down!"

"My God," I said. "Are you okay?"

"Yes, yes, I'm fine," she gasped, tears streaming down her

face. "I was just . . . so afraid . . . she was going to cover me with that rug!" I could barely discern her words through her laughter and my surprise. It was the first time I'd heard Mom laugh in months. It was the most I'd heard her say in weeks. I didn't even realize my jaw had dropped until Precious tried to cover it with sloppy, wet kisses.

"We fell down the goddamn stairs!" JoAnn hollered. "Isn't that beautiful?"

"Yes, JoAnn," said Mom. She dabbed her eyes with the knotted rug. "It certainly is."

"Jesus," said JoAnn, snuggling cozily into Mom's shoulder. "Are you hungry or what?"

"Starved," said Yvella. "You know, I'm beginning to think Michael and Alfred have forgotten about us."

"There ain't nobody here but us chickens!" JoAnn hooted. And then: "We fell down the goddamn stairs!" Which made both of them explode again in fresh gales of laughter.

After Michael and my grandfather finally returned with dinner, and for the rest of the evening, while passing the carrots or watching a movie, JoAnn and Yvella kept eyeing each other conspiratorially and collapsing in trills of giggles over their own private joke. It was a joke that proved very difficult to explain to Michael and Alfred, since the only point either of them seemed capable of absorbing was that I'd left Yvella and JoAnn unsupervised and allowed them to take a dangerous fall. Michael, in particular, seemed immune to my assurances that, for the first time, I felt certain that Mom was going to be okay.

The following morning, as we prepared to leave, my grandfather snipped pink roses for Yvella from his garden, and both my grandparents presented them to her ceremoniously as we loaded ourselves into the car for the slow drive back to Houston. "Screw the bastards," JoAnn said, embracing her. "You're beautiful!" she called after us as we pulled away, honking cattle out of the long, curving drive, and watching in the rearview mirror as my grandparents waved good-bye.

For the rest of the trip to Texas, Yvella seemed *that* much brighter. She actually spoke to Michael and me—not a lot, but when she did, she at least sounded like herself. "I let myself get so down," she said, somewhere around Texarkana. "I forgot that I had anything to look forward to." And every now and then, she'd start giggling again about having fallen down the stairs.

When we finally got back to Houston, Yvella literally collapsed in Michael's arms on the front lawn, sobbing in gratitude for the chance to return to her life, and I struggled to remove the Realtor's lock from her dilapidated and dearly loved front door.

EIGHT

Hello, I Must Be Going

As JoAnn's Alzheimer's advanced, the question I was most frequently asked by the people who love me was "Does she still remember who you are?" It was a question posed with the purpose of providing me with comfort, in order to offer me an opportunity to share "the worst" of the experience. As such, it was also a question that expressed one of the most basic anxieties we all share about love—that it's roving and ephemeral and absentminded. That the heart is as prone to one-night stands as the flesh. That we're all flashes in the pan of affection—out of sight, and out of mind. I was grateful to my friends and relatives for asking me this question. But whether or not JoAnn still remembered who I was seemed beside the point. The point being that I remembered who she was.

In the spring of 2008, four years after her initial diagnosis, JoAnn began experiencing greater difficulty performing basic tasks like eating and walking. By that point, Alfred was at wit's end and began to insist, during frantic phone calls, that he needed more than part-time help taking care of JoAnn. So Mother, freshly divorced from Peter Ickpudth, volunteered to travel to Tennessee, in order to organize the rounds of nurses and caretakers JoAnn required and to fill in the scheduling gaps herself. "You're sure you don't mind?" I asked Mother when she informed me of her plans.

"No," said Mother. "As much as it shocks me to say it, I don't mind a bit. In fact, God help me, I think I might actually enjoy spending a little time alone with my parents."

"Gee, give a fella a little warning, would you?" I said. "Next time, at least tell me to sit down first."

"If there ever is a next time, Robert," Mother said, "you have my solemn assurance that I will."

Of course, "filling in the scheduling gaps" doesn't begin to convey the reality of the work Mother had volunteered for, as anyone who's ever taken care of a person with Alzheimer's knows full well. Nighttime is the most difficult part of the day to staff, and also, quite often, the busiest. The punishing phenomenon known as "sundowning," in which people with Alzheimer's become increasingly subject to spells of anxiety in the night, means that caretakers often go sleepless and are never entirely off-duty, much like the parents of newborn children.

That June, Alfred had finally conceded that he could no longer help JoAnn upstairs. So Mother and I transformed their stately dining room into a makeshift bedroom. Seeing JoAnn and Alfred encamped in the middle of the house, dressed in their old-fashioned nightclothes and sleeping in their proper mahogany twin beds was not without its old-world charm, but it also provided a constant reminder of the centrality of JoAnn's illness within our lives. There was something naked and unsettling about seeing them down there, out of place, stripped of their matrimonial privacy. For the sake of JoAnn's safety, there was no way around it, but it felt like a violation.

There was a part of me that wanted to avert my eyes whenever I walked through the room—in order to protect their dignity, and in order to keep from seeing the truth.

In Nashville, Mother started her day by bringing my grandmother breakfast on a tray. After feeding her, she'd gently brush her hair, and tenderly apply makeup to her face with soft mink brushes. By this stage of my grandmother's illness, she often wore a look of surprise when she awoke in the mornings. And as Mother did her makeup, she seemed to coax her back into the world, to soothe her into consciousness. Mother insisted that JoAnn have her hair and makeup done every morning. In fact, she'd send me flying across Manhattan—from Bloomingdale's to Barneys and back again—with elaborate shopping lists of arcane moisturizers and astringents not to be found in the city of Nashville. "Believe you me," Mother told me, "they're as vital as any old medicine."

Watching my mother care for JoAnn with so much tenderness and delicacy, as my grandfather and I had done, I thought of many things. I thought about how deep superficiality can be, about how genuine artifice often is, and how tiny, workaday actions can add up to miracles. On the most literal level, my mother was just applying cosmetics, but in the big, rushing narrative of our lives, she was closing the circle, breaking the cycle, giving back to my grandmother everything JoAnn had given her as a little girl, and then some. Unpacking her cosmetics, Mother resembled a magician unloading a bag of tricks. As she worked, she'd speak softly to my grandmother. "Mama, now I'm lining your eyes . . . I'm rouging your cheeks . . . painting your lips. Remember when you taught me how to do this? When I was a little girl? Remember you taught me to dab my bottom lip just like that?"

It might seem hopelessly frivolous, this heightened concern with JoAnn's appearance, considering the increasing seriousness of her dementia. Soon, she was unable to recognize Mother or me at all and had great difficulty forming coherent sentences, but the further my grandmother slipped away, the more it mattered to us that she was treated like a person.

I desperately wanted to protect JoAnn—not so much from her disease, because to a certain extent, I'd made peace with Alzheimer's. But what I never managed to make peace with was the hideous way some people treated her when they thought she was batty or feebleminded. I couldn't bear to see her patronized, as though she were a small child, or condescended to, as though she were a fool. It robbed JoAnn of her humanity. To combat this, the finest arrow in our quiver, mother's and mine, was Maybelline—or better yet, Guerlain.

It was amazing to see how differently JoAnn was treated in public when her shoes matched her handbag, even if she was trying to lick paint off the Buick. In general, I have only one word of advice for any woman desiring to project an image of levelheaded sobriety, and that word is "accessorize." Accessorize, accessorize, accessorize. Just ask yourself, have you ever seen a bag lady with a Cartier brooch pinned to her sweater set? Or a madwoman with a Chanel camellia fastened to the shoulder of her bouclé suit? Of course you haven't. And do you know why? Because that kind of coordination requires advanced cognitive skills and a profound relationship with reality.

Remember how paranoid Nancy Reagan became about

Ronald Reagan's photo ops after he got Alzheimer's? So that you never saw him with less than a spit-shine polish, and that dreadful Howdy Doody makeup? Well, I used to roll my eyes at that sort of vanity until JoAnn got so sick, and then I realized two things. First, the power of fashion to divert attention from the way you act to the way you look. And second, the unshakable grip of the desire to protect those you love by managing appearances.

I've thought a lot about my grandmother seeming "surprised," toward the end of her life, by her surroundings when she first awoke to them in the mornings. I still don't know the nature of that surprise. It could just have been the same kind of disorientation that you experience when you wake up in a new apartment or hotel room, and it takes a minute for your memory to kick in and remind you where you are.

Or it could be that JoAnn was segueing into another kind of existence, and when she woke up and realized she was still on this mortal plane, it caught her by surprise. Sometime in those months, I talked to a psychic (I know, I know) about my grandmother's condition, and she, of all people, told me one of the only comforting things anybody said to me that year. She said, "Your grandmother isn't here anymore."

"What do you mean she's not here? She's not dead."

"No, she's not dead. But she isn't here, either."

"Then where is she? Cleveland? Baltimore?"

"She's everywhere."

I know that's not a revelatory bit of cosmology. But here's what it meant to me at the time. You know those terrible moves we all made when we were young and poor, and still in college, and once every six months or so we'd move from one lousy apartment to another lousy apartment, lugging our possessions in broken-down old liquor boxes scored from the grocery store, stuffed into the back of VW Bugs? You know how long it takes to move across town that way, one VW Bug-full at a time, hauling your worldly goods upstairs and down, perhaps with the help of a couple of friends similarly young and poor, whom you bribe with beer and pizzas? Well, it occurred to me after this exchange with the psychic that maybe *that,* in a metaphysical sense, was what was happening to my grandmother. Maybe we all enter "the next life" with the kind of youthful, overjoyed poverty we have when we're sixteen, mystified by the fresh independence we've been, all at once, granted. Maybe JoAnn, for the last couple of years, had been toting her "self" to the other side, one broken-down liquor box at a time. Maybe she'd begun with the fragile, most breakable items—her quicksilver wit and humor and intelligence. Maybe she'd moved those first because they were the first things she'd need in her next stage of existence.

I fear this is precisely the kind of literalist, wishful thinking that grieving people are prone to latch on to. It is, nevertheless, a comforting, hopeful notion. Apparently, some reporter once accused Patti Davis of spreading false hope by suggesting that stem-cell research might benefit Alzheimer's patients, to which she replied, "There's no such thing as false hope. That's the point of hope." Well, exactly.

So here's another hopeful thought. As that year progressed, JoAnn seemed to talk more and more to her loved ones who were dead and buried. "Who's she talking to?" one of her caretakers—a blond and buoyant woman infused with a burning religious fervor—asked me that spring. "Hmm, hard to say," I answered. "Her father, maybe?"

"He's not with us anymore, is he?" she asked.

"Well, he's not with you and me," I answered, "but he might be with her."

"Ah, yes," she said. "Some people believe that's a sign. Talking to the dead. That the closer a patient gets to death, the more they stop talking to the living and start talking to folks on the other side. Some people believe that, but I don't. Not sure it's Christian."

"So you'd prefer to think she's delusional?" I asked.

"Whatever you want to call it," she said.

"Well, if my options are believing that my grandmother is delusional or that she's really talking to her father, then I'll choose to believe she's talking to her father."

"Some people believe that way," the woman answered. "But I'm not sure it's Christian."

I am, likewise, uncertain of the heretical nature of this belief, but if my grandmother was accompanied, at this stage of her journey, by all her loved ones, the living and the dead, then it strikes me as being one of God's little mercies, one of those humble blessings that lines the path forward through sadness.

It was a season of little mercies: JoAnn talking to the dead, and Mother taking such care to coordinate JoAnn's outfits and how she spent her days. At night, they'd watch old Judy Garland musicals while Mother curled JoAnn's hair before tucking her into bed. Then Mother herself would fall asleep in a four-poster bed built for her by her father when she was a little girl. "Isn't my daughter the most remarkable woman?" my grandfather said whenever we talked on the phone. "I ask you, don't I just have the greatest daughter in the world?"

"So what?" you may be saying to yourself. "It's fairly normal for a dutiful daughter to care for her ailing mother."

Well, that's what was so stupendous about it. We'd never had "normal" before. This caretaking arrangement, so seemingly ordinary, would have been, at any other time of my life, far beyond the bounds of my imagination. To see Mother treat JoAnn like her own child—which in many ways, she'd become—was the most remarkable thing I've ever witnessed. (It also served as an object lesson in parenthood—namely, that parents should always keep in mind, before allowing relations with their children to devolve into conflict, that sooner or later, the diaper will be on the other tush.) It was miraculous that, for most of their lives, my mother and grandmother had seemed to loathe each other. Of course, I now believe that they always loved each other deeply and had just never made their relationship work. Nevertheless, for the better part of forty years, they'd given an extremely convincing impression of hatred. JoAnn seemed to find intimacy with her only child impossible. And Mother had focused an entire lifetime's worth of anger and bitterness and disappointment on JoAnn. But now, the past was, quite literally, forgotten.

It was a little jarring. All a little too good to be true. As perverse as it sounds, after a lifetime of conflict, having a family filled with peace and love and affection made me nervous, convinced that the other shoe would drop any minute. I mean, all our stars seemed to be aligning. Mother, to my great surprise, even settled into a relaxed new domesticity. Michael says that the first time he visited our house, the only things in our refrigerator were Coca-Cola and caviar. His experience was totally representative of my childhood, during which Mother almost single-handedly kept our local Chinese takeout joint afloat. In fact, looking back, I think I was the only kid in Texas who grew up eating more moo goo gai pan than barbecue. But while staying with her parents, Mother started, as she put it, "exploring the art of French cooking." And since she never does anything by halves, she flambéed everything for a month. During which time, she never served a meal without a near-explosion. Then she actually started gardening! And by gardening I mean she completely relandscaped my grandparents' property, adding an orchard and an English rose garden. "Oh, I just find gardening so relaxing," she told me over the phone. During the silence that followed, I groped desperately through my memory, trying to remember whether "I just find gardening so relaxing" was one of the telephone code phrases Mother and I had devised years ago to indicate the presence of an armed intruder in the house.

But as I fumbled for words, Mother said, "Besides, your grandmother likes to help me plant the bulbs. So, you know, it's something we can do together." And then, "Oh, hey, sweetie, let's talk later, okay? That's her calling me from the other room. I'll call you back after supper, all right? I'll report back how it goes. Tonight *everything's* a soufflé!"

At the end of 2008, I wrote an essay for *The New York Times* about the journey on which my grandmother's Alzheimer's had taken our family, wary of the response it would receive. I wanted to tell the truth about JoAnn's illness, that it had been an experience filled with sadness but also with such joy and laughter. But I was concerned that readers—and particularly those with firsthand experience of caring for a loved one with Alzheimer's—might mistake my meaning and believe I was making light of their challenges and suffering.

On the contrary, I received a staggering outpouring of letters from all over the world, filled with so many extraordinarily touching stories. One was from a woman who'd watched as her mother-in-law, whose son had been murdered years earlier, was finally able to forget the pain this tragedy had wrought, due to Alzheimer's. Another letter was from a lesbian whose mother had never been able to accept the truth of her life until Alzheimer's. Yet another was from a man whose father had survived the Holocaust and, regardless of his later accomplishments, had remained haunted by his past until Alzheimer's. "It was as if for the first time," this man wrote of his father, "the Alzheimer's had washed his mind clean, and the sweetness of his personality before the torture and murder altered it was able to come out. He was kind and loving in a way he could not be when the cruelty of mankind colored his personality. We had a relationship we would have otherwise never had and I was able to experience the truth of what he had once been." Reading these amazing letters, I realized that my family's experience wasn't entirely unique—that for many families, Alzheimer's, an unquestionably tragic disease, is not necessarily without its blessings.

One of the last parts of the brain to be affected by Alzheimer's holds poetry and music, which meant that my grandmother, at a time when she could remember very little else, could still sing the score of *Follow the Fleet*! She remembered all the words to that marvelous old Groucho Marx song "Hello, I Must Be Going," along with most of the Cole Porter songbook. She also knew a smattering of poetry she'd memorized over the years, including those lines by Aeschylus that Robert Kennedy used to quote, back when my grandmother had a big thing for Robert Kennedy. Over and over, JoAnn would recite: "And even in our sleep, pain that cannot forget / Falls drop by drop upon the heart. / And in our own despair, against our will / Comes wisdom to us by the awful grace of God."

"Jesus," Mother said, rubbing her temples, *"how many times* do we have to hear the Robert Kennedy thing? I mean, of all the broken records for her to get stuck on."

Mother had a point. Aeschylus wouldn't have been my special request, either, but those lines did pack a wallop of thematic resonance. Through the "awful grace" of JoAnn's Alzheimer's, we got more than wisdom. We got our family back.

It's difficult to overstate the impact my grandmother's Alzheimer's has had on my worldview, hard to articulate the extent of its influence on my thinking. The most basic conclusion it's prompted is that as long as you're alive, anything is possible. That sounds almost unbearably Pollyannaish, I know. It's embarrassing even to write. But I'm not striving for optimism here. What I mean is that since life has an agonizing tendency to offer us the best and the worst at the same time, to give us what we ask for in an utterly unforeseen form, even fairly predictable outcomes prove unrecognizable upon arrival. What I didn't understand, on those grim days when I believed JoAnn would be better off dead than living with this dread disease, was how much she had left to experience and how much I had left to learn.

I learned that one's cleverness can annihilate one's joy, kill it off completely. Just before Christmas of 2007, as we were decorating the tree, my grandmother gazed with wonder into the sparkling white lights, the red and gold glass balls, the tinsel and ribbon and presents. She was, without question, the happiest person in the room. The rest of us—Michael, Mother, Alfred, and I—were already sick to death of the holiday and all the drudgery that goes along with it. But one by one, we stopped to watch my grandmother's gorgeous smiling face marveling at the angel staring down at her and smelling the fresh, living fragrance of the fir tree. "Look at her," I remember thinking. "She's actually enjoying herself. She's present to the once-in-a-lifetime momentness of this in a way that no longer even occurs to me. In a way that I've forgotten. Which one of us," I said to myself, "could be said to be suffering an infirmity?" It's an experience that's remained with me, and that's prompted a series of thoughts, many of them religious. For instance, it's surely no coincidence that so many of the saints—like Bernadette of Lourdes or Juan Diego, to whom Mary was said to have appeared—were people considered dim or simple by their communities. Whether you consider those stories to be scriptural or mythological, it has to mean something that in them, the mother of God never appears to the class valedictorian. Maybe what these stories are trying to say is that illumination, the sacred, God, is right there— literally manifesting before us, only we can't see it because we're blinded by the prejudices of intellect. In the Bible, Jesus says, "The kingdom of heaven is within you"—a thought so enormous, I don't believe any of us can really comprehend it. ("Think of it," one of my college professors once said, pointing to my classmates one by one. "The kingdom of God is within *you*. And *you*. And *you*. Think of how differently you would treat one another if, for even one day, you really believed that heaven actually lived inside the person sitting beside you.")

Jesus also says, "It's harder for a rich man to enter the kingdom of heaven than it is for a camel to pass through the eye of a needle." Traditional readings of this passage always interpret it to mean, obviously, that material concerns distract people from pursuing salvation, that one can't serve God and Mammon. But the experience of my grandmother's Alzheimer's, and the amazing joy it brought her, caused another interpretation to occur to me. What if, when considering this passage, you substitute intellectual for material riches? What if you stop thinking of heaven as a geographical location beyond the pearly gates? What happens if heaven stops being the original gated community and becomes instead that kingdom of God that's within each of us—our own unfettered love and peace? What if it's only our commitment to being "smart" that prevents us from experiencing divine joy? From being plain old happy and present to all of life's little miracles.

Alzheimer's is often referred to as "a second childhood." It's a phrase that used to offend me, since it's often delivered with disrespect. But from another perspective, it can be pretty profound. When small children fall, they cry, and in five minutes they've forgotten all about it. This sort of resilience seems so impossible in adulthood, but my grandmother taught me the importance of forgetting. Now, I certainly understand that my grandmother suffered a debilitating, in many ways tragic, disease that relentlessly stripped her of cognitive ability, while I enjoy the blessing of perfect health. But I'm also very clear that throughout her Alzheimer's, my grandmother never stopped teaching me through the example of her life.

I've always been a person to whom "forgive and forget" has seemed absurdly unworkable. Though I'm not so arrogant as to presume to edit scripture, since witnessing my grandmother's Alzheimer's, I've begun to wonder whether a small reversal wouldn't better suit humanity. Maybe it would be more practical if forgetting preceded forgiving. Maybe happiness would be more easily achieved if we all made a practice of forgetting.

Mark Twain used to tell a story. The way I heard it, Twain claimed to have once been sick unto dying, when a doctor, summoned to his deathbed, told him, "Sorry, Mr. Twain, but you've got no hope."

"No hope?" he repeated. "You mean there's nothing to be done?"

"Of course there's something to be done," said the doctor. "You *could* give up drinking, smoking, and carousing all night. But you're not going to do that, so you've got no hope."

Contrary to all expectations, however, Mark Twain did, in fact, give up drinking, smoking, and carousing all night, and soon made a full recovery.

A few months later, though, his virtuous maiden aunt, a pillar of the church and local temperance society, fell desperately ill with the very same ailment and promptly died.

"You see," said Twain, "she had nothing to give up. The poor woman was like a sinking ship without cargo to cast overboard."

I've often thought of this story in relation to Alzheimer's, and it seems very likely that, as with my mother and grandmother, the survival of many relationships depends upon the ability to "give up" remembering.

Which is, often, exactly what we're most unwilling to do. Mostly because our memories, our histories, our versions of the past, seem so basic to our individual identities. We believe that the way we remember something is the truth that defines us. It's one of the principle fears of Alzheimer's, one of the reasons people so often say they'd rather die than have it. They think that if they develop Alzheimer's, they'll be forced to abandon them*selves* to oblivion.

I make no claims to know the true nature of identity, but the experience of my grandmother's Alzheimer's suggests to me that, whoever we are, we are not what we remember. In fact, in a certain sense, the opposite is true. It seems possible that your memories can prevent you from becoming who you really are. That an over-attachment to the past can actually prevent you from having a future. I'm certain, for instance, that my grandmother always loved my mother and that their shared history interfered with her ability to show it. But when Alzheimer's compelled JoAnn to let go of the past, she was finally (almost immediately) able to really be herself with her only child.

"Life cannot go on without much forgetting!" wrote Balzac. And that's the greatest thing my grandmother ever taught me—that there's something more absolute and basic than our biographies that defines us. Of course, it's somewhat threatening, as a writer, to realize that we are more than our stories. But as a person, it's liberating to consider that you are not the sum of your anecdotes; that some tiny, resilient bud of self persists inside you, even when you can't remember your own name.

And I'd like to think that bud of self is love. That was the last thing my grandmother was ever able to say. "I love you. It's beautiful. I love you."

A Legacy

I was in New York on the Sunday night in August 2010 when Mother called to say that JoAnn had died. The next morning, Michael and I flew to Nashville. Two days after that, Mother, Michael, and I flew to Houston, where a memorial service was held at St. Stephen's Episcopal Church, officiated with great kindness by the Reverend Lisa Hunt. Alfred was too ill to attend. He'd suffered a stroke that summer from which he hasn't recovered. As throughout his life, my grandfather still spends most days talking adoringly to his wife.

Yvella was also too ill to attend JoAnn's memorial service, though, in general, her fortunes have enjoyed a happy reversal since her return from Indiana. Recognizing her determination to remain in her house, Michael's sister Laurie and her family have moved in with Yvella, supported and cared for her. They have enriched her home with cash and bustle and babies. Thanks to them, Mom has finally been able to savor the prerogative of her age and station: the pleasure of companionship without the burden of worry and responsibility.

I was deliberately inconsolable on the day of JoAnn's service. "Don't cry," Michael comforted me on that stormy afternoon at St. Stephen's, with the torrid rain whipping through the weighty, somber branches of Houston's post oaks. "Your grandmother wouldn't want you to be so sad."

"Yes," I told him, "she would."

"No," he said. "I don't believe that."

"Michael," I said, from behind my handkerchief. "She *told* me she would."

"When?"

"Years ago, before she got sick. She told me."

"What did she say?"

"She said, 'On the day of my funeral I want you to be sad.' She said, 'Don't give me any of that loser Celebration of Life bullshit. I want *grief,* damn it. I want you to cry your little eyes out.'"

"I see," said Michael.

"It's always best," I wailed, "when the Loved One makes her final wishes known. So much simpler for the family."

As we left St. Stephen's, the rain sizzled and popped on the pavement; steam hissed off of puddles in the parking lot. Despite the determined angling of umbrellas, mourners' suits and dark silk dresses were soaked through by singeing drop-lets. Under the porte cochere, where Mother stood smoking a cigarette, a hot wind, like an exhaling furnace, nearly blew the wig right off her head. "That's Mama," she said, and nodded admiringly. While gripping on to her fake blond locks, Mother waved her menthol toward the raging sky. "All this *Omen* weather. It's all Mama. God, that woman could make an exit."

Like Alfred, I also spend my days talking to JoAnn. She is, if anything, more present to me now. When JoAnn was liberated from her body, I felt infused with her strength. I'm less frightened of things now. More certain, less patient.

But still, I miss her. I miss gossiping with her on the telephone and watching other people react to her, seeing their eyes widen with outrage and laughter. I guess all I'm saying is what Ezra Pound already wrote in that poem "In Durance": "I am homesick after mine own kind that know, and feel / And have some breath for beauty."

I am homesick for the way JoAnn could make a room look, and for the way her voice sounded, and for the pouty face she made in the mirror when she put on her lipstick. I miss her even though, as Pound writes, she swirls and calls and comes to me, "out of the mist of my soul . . . bearing old magic."

Oh JoAnn, nothing will ever be quite so funny again. And I am homesick after mine own kind.

ACKNOWLEDGMENTS

"All My Ever-Lovin' Gratitude . . ."

To my dearly beloveds, my darling family and friends who've given me happiness, sparkling like a diamond ring in a pale blue box.

To Michael, my mother and father, JoAnn, Alfred, Yvella, Jule, Ello, and KC. I'm not sure if I'm the luckiest man in the world because I have you, or if it's because I'm the luckiest man in the world that I got you in the first place. Anything marvelous about my life is utterly because of you.

To Tina Cafeo and Cindy Gratz, the best damn friends any boy could ever have: I'd be lost without you, and what's more, I wouldn't even want to find my way.

To Darrell Pucciarello, Heather Milliet, Glenda Leleux, Caroline Biggs, Manny Cafeo, Andrea Eisenstein Winard and Yosef, Donnette Heath, Eladia Causil-Rodriguez, Tiajuana Anderson Neel, Amira Gertz, Marilyn Bellock, Jim Rouen, Maggie Rouen, Harriet Hodges, Jennifer Connors, Kristy Johnson, Jessica Phillips and Scott Wright, Diane and Gene Cates, Marie Howe, Victoria Redel, Vance Muse, Jeanne Adams, Charlotte Coffelt, Muffie Moroney, Nadia Ackerman, Jody Klein, Benedicta Otalor Sisti, Henry Kaufman, Terra Layton, Adam Gibson, Joan Edwards, Annette Baker, Doug Harvey, Gary Esposito and Marisela and Dante, Blair McMorrow, Joanie Philpot, Doug Pashley, Tina Lopes, Joanne Brownstein, Lauren Millar, Jessica Bennington, Jeff and Beth Bowden, Robbie Ard, Ned Joyce, River Jordan, Donna Masini, Sarah Bird, Diane Wilson, Paul Lisicky, Paul Hochman, and Sigrid Nunez.

To Laurie, Christopher, Amelia, and Jasmine, my beautiful family.

To the scintillating Sue Schechter.

To the completely marvelous Honor Moore, who is always right about everything.

To glorious Janis Owens, for being my Eleanor Roosevelt and Julia Sugarbaker both at the same time.

To the all-knowing Dr. Wiaam Falouji.

To the venerable Vernon Caldera, a sight to behold to whom I am most beholden.

To Peggy, Jimmy, and Kay Curtis, Keri Schmidt, Kim Broom, and Eugenia Dennard: Oh, how I adore thee.

To Betty and Freck Fleming, and to Kathryn Ross, my godparents extraordinaire: You have my whole heart.

To Rena Shrum, simply a goddess.

To Kathy Patrick and the Pulpwood Queens, shining lights of literacy.

To Kathie Bennett and her mother, the invincible Barbara Wells Clemons.

To Marsha Toy Engstrom, a cheerleader and a champion.

To Sarah Lawrence College, a place that always was and will be the Emerald City.

To Suzanne Gardinier, Julie Abraham and Amy Schrager Lang, Lyde Sizer, Rose Anne Thom, Sarah Brice Lynch, Thyra Briggs, and Heather McDonnell.

To darling Darla McCorkle, Hugh, Atticus, and Delilah:

Thank you for the beds, the love, the friendship, and the jokes. Darla, you're one of *the* special people of all time.

To Michael Deleget, a great artist and the only man I'd ever drive to East Haddam, Connecticut, for. Once.

To *The Texas Observer* and my family there. Most especially, brilliant Bob Moser, Brad Tyer, and Ruth Pennebaker.

To my marvelous *Lonny* friends: Michelle Adams, Patrick Cline, Ellie Somerville, Max McDonnell, Kari Costas, Shawn Gauthier, Amber Lindros, and Isa Salazar.

To the Rothko Chapel, the most reverent, holy place I know.

To Emilie Farenthold, Dorothy Slater-Brown, Joslin Kryjcir, Mary Ann Bruni, Martha Claire Tompkins, Gayle DeGeurin, and Emilee Whitehurst, for being so completely lovely and giving me some of the happiest evenings of my life.

To Gail Hochman, gorgeous human and great agent.

To George Witte, best man and world's finest editor.

To John Karle, who makes me sound so much better than I really am.

To the good, good folks of Brandt & Hochman and St. Martin's Press.

And to Sissy Farenthold, who showed me, through her own shining example, that it is possible for life to get better and better and better. You're not only the gold standard of people, you're also a hell of a lot of fun. I love you.

Oh, and one more thing. Michael said this fabulous thing. He said, "The thing about the women in your family is that they're ladies, yes, but they're also badasses." Perfection. And so, finally, to all the beautiful badass ladies, may they reign in splendor.